To the lads with the badges

Matrix Revelations

A thinking fan's guide to the *Matrix* trilogy

Edited by Steve Couch

www.damarispublishing.com

Copyright © 2003 the Damaris Trust

The authors assert the moral right to be identified as the authors of this work.

First edition published in 2003 by
Damaris Publishing
PO Box 200, Southampton, Hampshire, SO17 2DL
www.damarispublishing.com

ISBN 1-904753-01-9

A catalogue record for this book is available from the British Library
Designed and typeset by AD Publishing Services Limited
Printed and bound in Great Britain by Bookmarkque Ltd, Croydon, Surrey

Contents

Introduction

My local multiplex likes to go the extra mile in making it seem like they care. The staff are referred to as 'cast members' and wear badges that show not only their names, but also their favourite film. We tried to persuade one of my friends, a film enthusiast, to apply for a job there just so that we could see how they reacted to him opting for *The Battleship Potemkin*. Anyway, somewhere between 1999 and 2000 something interesting started to happen. A high proportion of the staff (mostly young males) all started claiming the same film as their favourite: *The Matrix*.

The Matrix came out in 1999, but owes much of its following to the subsequent video and DVD releases. By the time *The Matrix Reloaded* (2003) and *The Matrix Revolutions* (2003) arrived, they were among the most keenly awaited films of recent times (and this, let's not forget, during an era of high profile franchises such as *The Lord of the Rings* and *Harry Potter*). Its combination of complex sci-fi storyline, state of the art special effects and philosophical musing has drawn in a wide and diverse audience – far broader than the teenage lads working at my local multiplex might suggest. Some of those fans come for the action and have no interest in the thought behind the films – it isn't the question that drives you if all you want is a car chase followed by a punch up.

But others have delved deeply into the *Matrix* universe, grappling to understand as much as they can. The Internet is full of discussion boards where fans posted their own favourite theories as to where the trilogy would go after *Reloaded*. One of the more impressive ones, which was detailed enough to have you believing it just might be the real deal, was that the war had long since ended and the humans had won. In this version, the humans from Zion were really machines reprogrammed to believe they were humans, and the power plants of Zion that Hamann and Neo discuss in *Reloaded* are actually providing power for the human cities on the surface of the Earth. There are countless other ideas, and perhaps the Wachowskis would do well to tap into them, inviting script submissions for a second volume of *The Animatrix*, featuring alternative endings to their trilogy. But however persuasive these alternative endings may have been at the time (part of me is still drawn to the idea of Persephone as the mother of the Matrix, but don't get me started) the Wachowskis chose the conclusion to their tale for a reason – it helped to tell their story and to serve the philosophical argument they have been conducting through the silver screen.

Some critics have dismissed the trilogy, particularly *Reloaded* and *Revolutions*, for failing to answer any of the questions it poses. They condemn the films as pretentious and not nearly as clever as the Wachowskis would like us to think they are. We disagree. We may hold a different worldview to the Wachowskis and come to different conclusions about the issues they tackle in the films, but there is definitely some cohesive, serious thought behind the films.

This book is for fans of the films who want more than just the action. It is written by fans of the films with a view to helping people to understand the films a little bit better. Not just to understand the twists and turns of plot, but also to get to grips with some of the concepts that have inspired the Wachowski brothers, and which drive their three-part masterpiece. Part One of the book concerns itself primarily with the films themselves. Part Two tackles some of the issues that underpin the trilogy. Obviously there is a degree of overlap, but generally the first half of the book raises questions which the second half answers more fully.

We have consciously tried to write for a general (rather than expert) audience – the only assumption that we have made is that by picking up this book you are interested in understanding serious concepts. We have tried to make the philosophy accessible without dumbing down or misrepresenting. Readers who want more detail are advised to try some of the books listed in the bibliography. Where we refer to websites, the details given are accurate at the time of writing, although it is possible that some links may become obsolete over time.

Some of the authors of this book share office space, and we've spent hours arguing over the meaning of particular lines of dialogue, the implication of specific frames and images, and the significance of character names. We haven't always reached a common mind on every subject, so the views of any one writer should not necessarily be taken to represent all of us – there are even places where a careful reading of the book will identify some of our differences. Nevertheless, the book as a whole is a collaborative affair, with chapters being read and commented on by several contributors as part of the editing process. Despite this, it is still the case that you should credit the named writer (or writers) of any chapter with anything that you enjoy, while leaving the blame for any glitches in the matrix with me as editor.

There are a number of individuals who are owed a debt of thanks, and this seems as good a place as any to pay up. Marcus Honeysett offered helpful comments on an early draft of chapter 7, and Andrew Glass, Sanskrit advisor on *The Matrix Revolutions* (how many films boast that job in the credits?) was extremely helpful in providing the sources and translations you will find in chapter 12. Julian Weisserhorn (the owner of the mythical *Battleship Potemkin* badge) helped us to prepare the final text, and the staff of AD Publishing saw the book through the final practicalities at breakneck speed. Various family members and friends of the contributors are also owed thanks for putting up with seeing less of their loved ones than they might have liked as we worked to finish things off. Finally, we should thank the other inhabitants of the Damaris office for their support and for putting up with the way this project has threatened, like Agent Smith, to take over everything else they were trying to do.

The process of watching and rewatching the films that writing this book has entailed has been (as you can imagine) a thoroughly enjoyable one. Although we have been working to a ludicrously tight schedule (I am writing this two days before our final copy deadline and less than two weeks since the cinematic release of *Revolutions*), we've found that the more we have watched and analysed the films, the more we have found to admire. We hope that in reading our book, you gain a similar appreciation of the *Matrix* trilogy, arguably the most significant series of films for many years. So sit down, relax and see just how deep the rabbit hole goes.

Steve Couch, November 2003

CHAPTER I

The architects

by Caroline Puntis and Peter S. Williams

*They are the gatekeepers. They are guarding all
the doors, they are holding all the keys.*

We don't know a lot about Larry and Andy Wachowski, the writers and directors of the *Matrix* trilogy. They keep their cards close to their chests and let their work do the talking. But if we want to understand the *Matrix* films, our search for answers will lead us to the mysterious pair, and to the rich panoply of influences that have shaped their masterpiece.

Who are the Wachowski brothers?

Larry and Andy Wachowski were born in Chicago in the 1960s to parents Ronald and Lynne. They both dropped out of good colleges and made a living from carpentry. These humble facts provide few clues as to how the brothers came to create the *Matrix* universe. As their biography on *The Matrix* DVD states, 'Little else is known about them.' Their path is best traced through the wealth of culture in which they have immersed themselves – a path that led them from comic books to screenplays and finally to directing.

A few snippets of information remain from the time before the Wachowski brothers decided to have a 'no press' clause written into their contracts. Clearly there was no need for more publicity following the success of

The Matrix. According to their producer, Joel Silver, they had another simple reason: 'They don't want to explain their thinking. They want the audience to find it.'[1]

What is *The Matrix*? Philosophical science fiction with lots of guns

To which genre of filmmaking does *The Matrix* belong? For all its groundbreaking progress in cinematic technology, the trilogy draws from many diverse types of film, rather than defining a new genre. Perhaps it sits most squarely in the sci-fi bracket, with its blend of speculation about the future, action and machines. However, there are elements of the Spaghetti Western, Hong Kong action, Japanese animation, Hollywood epic ... it is not a romantic comedy.

The Wachowskis have said that their main goal with *The Matrix* was to make an intellectual action movie: 'We like action movies, guns and kung fu, but we're tired of assembly-line action movies that are devoid of any intellectual content. We were determined to put as many ideas into the movie as we could.'[2] To help Keanu Reeves (Neo) to understand the ideas behind their cinematic vision, the brothers gave him a reading list including scientist Kevin Kelly's *Out of Control: The New Biology of Machines, Social Systems and the Economic World,*[3] and philosopher Jean Baudrillard's *Simulacra and Simulation*: 'I had to read Baudrillard,' says Reeves, 'I had to read *Out of Control* which is

---

[1] *Empire* magazine, June 2003, p.93.

[2] Christopher Probst, 'Welcome to the Machine', *American Cinematographer*, 80.4 (April 1999), p.32.

[3] Kevin Kelly is executive editor of *Wired* magazine.

about systems, evolutions, robots. And then there was another book that was about evolutionary psychology.'[4]

The *Matrix* films are at their best when their ground-breaking combination of dream-like aesthetics,[5] wire-aided kung-fu action and computer generated special effects are the indispensable means through which underlying philosophical questions are explored, rather than when that task is left to the dialogue alone. It is the combination of ideas with action that enables *The Matrix* to act, as executive producer Andrew Mason phrases it, as 'a mechanism for prodding an ignorant or dulled mind into questioning as many things as possible.'[6]

Science fiction has always been the perfect genre for exploring philosophical and religious questions, especially questions about humanity's relationship with the technology it produces. C. S. Lewis (who authored a science fiction trilogy of his own[7]) commented that science fiction is the only genuine consciousness-expanding drug! As Anthony Thacker explains:

> ... the striking thing about science fiction at the turn of the millennium is that the old gap between SF and religion has changed radically. There's been a discovery – maybe a rediscovery, that real faith sparks issues and tensions that can play out well in a sci-fi context. What's more, the best SF

---

[4] *Empire* magazine, June 2003, p.74.

[5] The films include many common motifs associated with dreams. For example, things happening in slow motion, repeated running down corridors and shifts of perception and scene.

[6] Christopher Probst, *op cit*, p.23.

[7] C. S. Lewis, *Out of the Silent Planet* (Bodley Head, 1938); *Perelandra* (Lane, 1943); *That Hideous Strength* (Lane, 1945).

raises questions about 'life, the universe and everything,' often in a striking way.[8]

It has been observed that: 'What makes *The Matrix* unique is its integration of various elements of the science fiction pantheon in a startling new way – the reality paradox, evil artificial intelligence, virtual reality, and, of course, lots of firepower.'[9]

There is an argument, however, that the Wachowskis' trilogy is not a true member of the science fiction camp. Joe Haldeman insists that *The Matrix* is 'sci-fi', which he refers to as science fiction's bastard child. Whereas a good science fiction movie may be short on plot and slow in pace, 'sci-fi needs action, thrills, a strong plot. Sci-fi movies want visual novelty, particularly mind-blowing special effects ... Good science fiction ... needs ideas and good writing.'[10] Furthermore, he adds that 'sci-fi in general is closer to myth than science fiction is. Its stories tend to be quests, involving supernatural powers and beings.'[11] Whether or not this argument can legitimately be applied to the *Matrix* films, the trilogy does nevertheless draw upon the themes of such science fiction classics as: *2001: A Space Odyssey* (1968), *Blade Runner* (1982), *The Terminator* (1984) and William Gibson's Cyberpunk novel *Neuromancer* (1984). Gibson's influence on the Wachowskis is reflected by the fact that he wrote a foreword to the

---

[8] Anthony Thacker, *A Closer Look at Science Fiction: discerning the spiritual quest of Star Trek, Babylon 5, Doctor Who, The X-Files and more* (Kingsway, 2001), p.11-12.

[9] James Gunn, 'The Reality Paradox in *The Matrix*' in *Taking the Red Pill: Science, Philosophy and Religion in The Matrix*, Glenn Yeffeth (ed.), p.83.

[10] Joe Haldeman, '*The Matrix* as Sci-Fi' in *Exploring the Matrix: Visions of the Cyber Present*, Karen Haber (ed.) (St. Martin's Press, 2003), p.174.

[11] *ibid.*

shooting script of *The Matrix*. In his own work, Gibson uses the term 'matrix' to refer to a virtual world.

The trilogy's trinity of interests

Over the years I've had to revise my notions of where I 'get' my ideas. Or is it that they get me? I think that ideas are huge things; bigger than me ... I don't much care about being a solo artist with original ideas. I care about being awake. Awake to Dream. I believe we collaborate with the idea wave; with past, present and future dreams.
RICK BERRY[12]

Larry and Andy Wachowski have always been open about the many and varied influences that helped them to shape *The Matrix* universe. Many of us will think that we recognise influences – they must have read this or seen that. As one fan asked, 'So, *was* the Japanese animation *Megazone 23* an inspiration for *The Matrix*? The stories seem very similar.' To which one of the Wachowski brothers replied, 'I've never seen it. But send us a copy, it sounds good.'[13] The truth is that sometimes different filmmakers come up with similar ideas at the same time, which may tap into a 'big idea'.

The Wachowskis' interests, as displayed in *The Matrix*, can be grouped into three overlapping categories: philosophical, religious and visual. Philosophically, the films raise and explore questions about knowledge, reality, consciousness, freedom, purpose, and our symbiotic relationship with technology.

---

[12] Rick Berry, 'Dreaming Real', in *Exploring the Matrix*, p.261.
[13] *Matrix Virtual Theatre*, 6th November 1999, www.warnervideo.com /matrixevents/wachowski.html

The Matrix has even been called 'a graduate thesis on consciousness in the sheep's clothing of an action adventure flick.'[14] Religiously, the Wachowskis deftly draw upon the symbolism of several different (and mutually exclusive) religious traditions: especially ancient Greek polytheism, Christianity, Gnosticism and Buddhism. Visually, *The Matrix* fuses influences from comic strips, Japanese animation, and Hong Kong martial arts films.

The Hollywood angle

For all the trilogy's alternative influences and independent aplomb, the boys from Chicago have still created a work that is marked by Hollywood. No doubt the Sydney shoot, free from the presence of harassed Hollywood executives, allowed the Wachowskis more creative control than they would have had back in LA. The brothers even customised the opening Warner Bros. ident with the phosphorescent green that characterises the world of the Matrix to symbolise their independence from 'the system' – but the fact remains that this trilogy was financed by Hollywood with certain expectations.

The trilogy is not short on classic plot twists, and has much that fits the framework of the typical Hollywood blockbuster. At the end of *The Matrix* the hero dies, only to be brought back to life by the kiss of the woman who loves him. All the loose ends seem to be convincingly tied up by the end of the first instalment. The central question – 'what is the Matrix' – has been answered.

[14] Read Mercer Schuchardt, 'What is the Matrix?' in *Taking the Red Pill: Science, Philosophy and Religion in The Matrix*, Glenn Yeffeth (ed.) (Summersdale, 2003), p.20.

However, this satisfaction is well and truly displaced during *The Matrix Reloaded* as the question takes on another layer of meaning. When Neo uses his powers outside of the Matrix, the reality of Zion is no longer certain – is it all just another layer of computer generated illusion? The cliffhanger ending fuelled Internet discussions for several months as we all waited for the exact nature of this complicated universe to be revealed in *The Matrix Revolutions*. When it arrived, however, this final part seemed to pose even more questions – a departure in Hollywood terms. Nevertheless, by the end of the first film in the franchise Neo is clearly established among the ranks of one of the most enduringly popular archetypes of modern cinema – the superhero.

The comic strip connection

For years, the superhero has enjoyed success in the pages of countless comic strips, making the transition to live action with varying degrees of success. Looking at Neo as he soars into the sky at the end of the first film, it is evident that the Wachowskis had every intention of developing the superhero myth through their trilogy. Since Superman first flew across our screens, film industry technology has made incredible advances. By the time the Wachowskis went into production, the ability to create a realistic superhero was within reach. As *Empire* magazine observed: 'the Wachowskis invented virtual actors because what the brothers really wanted, above everything else, was a superhero.'[15] Bearing a resemblance to Superman, Neo's characteristics certainly qualify him to take up the superhero mantle.

[15] *Empire* magazine, June 2003, p.90.

He is the strong, silent type, guileless in the face of conniving villains, tortured by his calling, and capable of a deep love that will always conflict with his commission to save the world.

The relationship of *The Matrix* with comic strips is far more than a mere nod to the modern superhero – it is fundamentally grounded in their aesthetic. During the 1990s, the Wachowski brothers penned stories for Marvel Comics, such as *Ectokid*. The story goes that in 1992, a friend of the brothers asked them to come up with an original concept for a comic book – the *Matrix* trilogy was born. Later, it was the storyboards of comic strip artists Steve Skroce and Geof Darrow that finally enabled Warner Bros. executives to catch the vision and hand over the reigns to two little-known directors.

The choice of visual framing made by the Wachowskis often reflects this comic-book origin; for example when a policeman attempts to handcuff Trinity at the beginning of *The Matrix*, we see him approaching her from behind as the camera looks through a frame formed by her hands-on-head, face-the-wall stance. Again, despite their inherently kinetic medium, one of the Wackowskis' most obvious stylistic signatures is the way they present us with momentary, and yet dynamic, comic-book style tableaux. It is a visual style that leaves the viewer with a series of specific and powerful 'images' imprinted upon the memory: Trinity hanging in mid-air before drop-kicking a cop; Neo firing an assault rifle in each hand while cartwheeling across the lobby; Morpheus being hit by a bullet as he runs through a water-drenched room towards Neo and Trinity's waiting helicopter. Each of these stand-out moments of action is the cinematic equivalent of a single comic-book frame. A well-drawn comic-book frame manages to be dynamic despite its inability to change, whereas a great moment from *The Matrix* manages to be almost static in the memory, despite the inability of film *not* to change.

Phone booths, sunglasses and mirrors

The visual impact of the Wachowskis' movies is enhanced considerably by certain borrowed motifs. These may play with the viewer's thirst for nostalgia, or, for certain individuals, knowledge of contemporary culture. For example, the prominence of phone booths immediately connects with the collective memory of Superman's legendary costume changes. Here, they are used to take minds out of the Matrix, but the issue remains the same – there's never a phone booth around when you need one!

Occasionally, the Wachowskis make blatant use of a visual concept. Paul di Filippo is convinced that the scene in which Neo's lips are sealed together during the interrogation with Agent Smith is a direct swipe from science fiction literature: 'Any viewer who knows Harlan Ellison's *I Have No Mouth, and I Must Scream* (1967), which recounts the Dantesque trials of humans trapped in the bowels of a sentient computer named AM, will appreciate this reference.'[16] Di Filippo also cites Samuel R. Delaney's *Nova* (1968) as a primary influence, particularly for his 'introduction to the concept of "spinal sockets", a method of cyborgization whereby humans may jack into and operate machinery and sensors.'[17] Before the Wachowskis could get their creative hands on this idea, however, it was used to

---

[16] Paul di Filippo, 'Literary Influences on The Matrix' in *Exploring the Matrix*, p.93
[17] *ibid.*

great effect in *Ghost in the Shell*, one of the animated Japanese features that the brothers declared essential viewing for members of the cast. With their shiny black leather outfits, black hair and flashy sunglasses, the characters obviously had an impact on the overall look for *The Matrix*, and in particular Trinity.

The use of reflective surfaces and mirrors assists the telling of the story as much as it provides another dimension visually. Artist Dean Motter says that 'Urban architecture relies on reflecting surfaces ... This is one way a society looks at itself. Mirrored structures obviously create the illusion of more space. It's the oldest trick in the book.'[18] The Wachowskis' reference to Lewis Carroll's *Alice Through the Looking Glass* is entirely appropriate for the turn of the twenty-first century. As the properties of the red pill start to take effect, Neo touches a mirror that appears to turn to liquid. The flowing silver makes its way up his arm until it has a stranglehold – Neo is almost stifled by that which held the image of himself, the very stuff of the Matrix, before he wakes up in the liquid environment of his pod. The first part of the trilogy alone positively shimmers with reflections. From the twin images of Neo in Morpheus' sunglasses as he decides which pill to take, to his distorted reflection in the Oracle's doorknob, to the exploding mirrored walls of an unknown corporate skyscraper – life in the Matrix is presented in images, underlining the question of what is real.

Trench coats, guns and kung fu

What the Wachowskis have achieved in combining their

[18] Dean Motter, 'Alice in Metropolis or It's All Done with Mirrors' in *Exploring the Matrix*, p.141.

favourite aspects of literature and film is the overall impression that what you are watching is incredibly cool. Writer Karen Haber says: '*The Matrix* is a glorious, triumphant celebration of style, wallowing in all of those guilty pleasures: speed, smarts, separate-but-equal trench coats, dark glasses, superpowers, paranoia and, oh, yes, don't forget the guns. If anyone has ever been guilty of making guns sexy, it's the Wachowskis.'[19]

The brothers are clearly fans of director John Woo.[20] His film *Face/Off* (1997) exemplifies the kind of action sequences that the Wachowskis pay tribute to in their trilogy. Woo's mastery of gravitas is often felt through a trench coat swirling in slow motion as another highly charged battle scene commences. The Wachowskis emulate these visual flourishes with an injection of humour – as Neo sets off the metal detector in the lobby scene, he opens his trench coat to reveal a literal coat of arms ... let the action begin. This scene in particular is a showcase for all things Wachowski – wire work, guns, music and speed ... in slow-mo.

Elsewhere, there are combat scenes that do away with guns and embrace the intricacies and elegance of kung fu. Legendary martial arts choreographer Woo-Ping Yuen directed the action which, combined with the 'bullet time' technique, is a veritable work of art. The brothers were convinced that Woo-Ping was their man having fallen for his genius in *Fist of Legend* (1994). He only agreed to join the production when it was promised that the four key 'American' actors would commit to four months of training before the shoot

[19] Karen Haber, 'Reflections in a Cyber Eye' in *Exploring the Matrix*, p.215.
[20] www.warnervideo.com/matrixevents/wachowski.html

started. Andy Wachowski says that their story is about 'robots versus kung fu'.[21]

The anime factor

Laurence Fishburne was asked to watch three Japanese anime[22] films, *Ghost in the Shell* (1995), *Akira* (1988) and *Ninja Scroll* (1995), as part of his preparation for the role of Morpheus. Part of the Wachowskis' dream was to bring the genre to life with real actors and real action.

The main parallels in *Ninja Scroll* are stylistic: samurai warriors leap, seemingly suspended in mid-air, whilst dispatching multiple foes, with obvious parallels to the gravity-defying action scenes in *The Matrix*. At one point a killer swarm of bees evokes the impending attack of the Sentinels in Zion. However, it is the content of *Akira* and *Ghost in the Shell* that shed most light on the Wachowskis' intentions for the *Matrix* trilogy.

The dingy back streets and fizzing lights from the first scene of *Akira* immediately conjure up the dark underworld of *The Matrix*. This is Japan in 2019 following World War III. Neo Tokyo is a dangerous place to be, with riots and heavy-handed military patrols. Kaneda, who wears the emblem of a pill capsule in two colours, leads a motorbike gang. As they race along a disused highway, his friend Tetsuo crashes into a

---

[21] 'Making the Matrix', *The Matrix* DVD (1999).

[22] Gloria Goodale says that this brand of Japanese animation (also known as 'Japanimation' or anime) has a number of features: 'Anime generally has complex storylines, with detailed characters who routinely discuss life-and-death matters such as religion and the afterlife. The figures are usually drawn with oversize eyes reflecting the Japanese belief that the eyes are the windows of the soul.' ('Japan's anime master makes powerful films', *Christian Science Monitor*, 29 October, quoted in Brian McLaren, 'Postmodern Stew' in *The Gospel Reloaded*, Chris Seay and Greg Garrett (eds) (Pinion Press, 1999), p.33.)

mysterious child. Instantly military officials arrive and take Tetsuo and the child away, despite Kaneda's protestations.

The child is one of three psychics, possibly representing the next stage in human evolution, and has escaped from an experimentation centre. There had been a fourth child, Akira, whose enormous power had effectively wiped out the old Tokyo in something resembling an atomic explosion. Tetsuo now has powers on a similar scale to Akira.

The military are determined to keep Tetsuo under control by locking him up. As his will to escape increases, so does Tetsuo's power. The girl psychic explains that the power of Lord Akira is within everyone, and that once it has been awoken you have to choose whether to use it for good or bad. The children and Akira choose to work for good ends, but Tetsuo uses his power negatively. In a scene that is reminiscent of the ultimate battle between Neo and Agent Smith in *The Matrix Revolutions*, the children go head-to-head with Tetsuo. His power eventually spirals out of control and the children summon up the spirit of Akira. Another 'atomic' dome of light, power and destruction sweeps through Tokyo, consuming the power of Tetsuo and the body of Kaneda. Tetsuo survives in an unknown form. The children want to rescue Kaneda, but only see two options – saving the boy could mean sacrificing themselves. Similarly, when Neo is presented with only two doors of choice by the Architect, he wants to believe there is another way. The girl explains their dilemma: 'We know the future doesn't necessarily proceed along a single course. There ought to be a future we can choose. It's up to us to find it.'

Ghost in the Shell, based on the manga[23] by Masamune Shirow, is set in Hong Kong in the near future. The film explores the increasingly complicated relationship between man and machine in a computerised age. It is not hard to see how the Wachowskis borrowed from this visual feast, from the computer screen titles to the back-of-the-head data sockets. The famous lobby scene in *The Matrix* is unmistakably a development of the climactic battle, that sees bullets tearing through concrete pillars and a cartwheeling woman dressed in black.

Major Kusanagi is a female cyborg working to bring a notorious hacker in for questioning. Known as the Puppet Master, he is a particularly clever 'ghost hacker' – someone who is capable of breaking through security barriers to penetrate the very soul, or ghost, of a cyborg. Cyborgs are composed of living human brain cells and synthetic bodies, known as shells. (Following the death of actress Gloria Foster, the Oracle in *The Matrix* and *The Matrix Reloaded*, the Wachowskis introduced the term 'shell' in *The Matrix Revolutions* to account for her new body.) The Major is incredibly strong and agile – her jet-black hair and blue eyes certainly compare to Trinity's, as do her acrobatic, kung fu and gun skills. The Puppet Master hacks into people's ghosts, implanting simulated experiences that enable him to control their actions. For those who have had their ghosts decimated by a hacker, there is little hope of recovering original memories. This leads Kusanagi's colleague, Bateau, to reflect, 'That's all it is – information. Even a simulated experience or a dream ... Any

[23] Manga are 'graphic novels' native to Japan, but now common in much of Asia. Visually, they are similar to western comic strips.

way you look at it, all the information that a person accumulates in a lifetime is just a drop in the bucket.'

Kusanagi is troubled by the question of her humanity – is it only because she is treated like a human being that she experiences life as a human? If a cyborg brain could generate its own ghost, its own essence, what would be the importance of being human? The Puppet Master's true nature is unclear. Is he a real person? A computer program? A bug? When, transferred into the shell of the Major, he finally has the opportunity to speak for himself, he reveals that he is a sentient being – a living, thinking entity created in a sea of information. Although he could copy himself, he believes that the organic properties of reproduction and dying are essential to his existence. He proposes a merger with the Major, hoping to create something new that will elevate their consciousness to a higher plane and enable them to become a part of all things.

In the penultimate scene, Kusanagi explains the new nature of her being to Bateau: 'When I was a child, my speech, feelings and thinking were all those of a child. Now that I am a man I have no more use for childish ways. And now I can say these things without help in my own voice. Because I am now neither the woman who was known as the Major, nor the program called the Puppet Master.' This speech borrows heavily from the thirteenth chapter of Paul's first letter to the Corinthians,[24] where he uses the child-to-man metaphor to explain the fullness of spiritual knowledge that will ultimately be his in eternity. As Kusanagi contemplates her future after leaving Bateau, she asks, 'And where

[24] 1 Corinthians 13:11-12.

does the newborn go from here?' In the same way, we wonder what will become of Neo at the end of *The Matrix Revolutions*. Perhaps her answer gives us a clue to his fate, in whatever form he now takes: 'The Net is vast and infinite.'

The question of consciousness

Anime is by no means the only form of cinema to concern itself with consciousness. As Clive Thorne points out: 'The issue of the nature of consciousness has been a recurrent theme in science fiction since the beginning of the genre [especially] the possibilities of conscious, self-aware machines ... By incorporating fictional technology that can make just about anything possible, science fiction can provide the vehicle for interesting philosophical thought experiments ...'[25] *The Matrix* raises the question of consciousness through its vision of a world where man-made artificial intelligences have become the dominant life-form. In this sense, *The Matrix* is a re-imagining and development of the story of Dr Frankenstein's monster.

From *2001: A Space Odyssey* to the *Terminator* movies, autonomous artificial intelligences, and the dangers that result from their existence, have loomed large on the big screen. Science fiction writers are quick to ask what happens when the created becomes more powerful, more intelligent, or more destructive than its creator. Sometimes, as in Kubrick and Spielberg's collaboration *AI: Artificial Intelligence* (2001), the original Frankenstein conceit is retained, with a sympathetic treatment of the 'monster', who

[25] Clive Thorne, 'Consciousness and Science Fiction': www.damaris.org/dcscs/readingroom/2000/scifi.htm

suffers at the hands of fearful ignorant humans. More often, the artificial intelligence is portrayed as a menace threatening the blameless humans, whose only offence has been to open a Pandora's box of new technology. Interestingly, the *Matrix* films tread something of a middle course, with both human and machine ranks including those who are open to harmony and co-oper-ation, as well as those who are closed to the possibility of anything other than all out conflict and victory over the enemy.

Conclusion

It would probably take half a lifetime to catch up on every book, comic, film and idea that has had an impact on the Wachowskis' filmmaking – the influences, refer-ences, nods and homages would no doubt become very evident. Knowledge of the main influences undoubtedly adds a fresh layer of appreciation to the films, but the *Matrix* trilogy is more than capable of standing on its own feet. Whether or not you know kung fu, sci-fi, anime and comic books as well as the Wachowskis, the films still pack a powerful flo-mo'd punch. Nothing can deny the Wachowskis their distinctive, much imitated, but still unique vision. As artists, they have done their homework. Their trilogy has not been released into a vacuum – they compliment and complement their sources. And they have started a revolution in the pres-entation of big ideas on the big screen.

CHAPTER 2

Down the rabbit hole: *The Matrix*

by Steve Couch

Wake up Neo ...

1999 was meant to mark the triumphant return of the *Star Wars* franchise. But *The Phantom Menace* disappointed and film fans looking for the magic of the first *Star Wars* movies soon realised that they had to look beyond George Lucas. The true successor to *Star Wars* (1977) turned out to be a lot like the original – an unheralded science fiction film that blew the audience's mind. A film unlike anything that had gone before. A film called *The Matrix*.

There are lots of ways to enjoy *The Matrix*. You can watch it for the action – the chases, the martial arts and gunfights. You can be amazed by the groundbreaking special effects – the now infamous and much copied bullet-time and flo-mo. You can thrill at the cool and sex appeal of the main characters – Laurence Fishburne as the enigmatic Morpheus, Carrie-Anne Moss as the steely-eyed Trinity, and the unexpected success of Keanu Reeves in a career-defining performance as Neo. If all you want from a film is a couple of hours of adrenaline rush, a sensory treat before returning to what we think of as reality, then *The Matrix* delivers in spades. If that's what you want from a movie, just swallow the blue pill, sit back and enjoy. Believe whatever you want to believe.

But then there's the rest. *The Matrix*, possibly more than any other major film (certainly any other mass appeal blockbuster) is stuffed full of ideas. Serious philosophical concepts underpin all of the action, driving the film on (Trinity is right – it is the question that drives us). For moviegoers who choose the red pill, who accept the Wachowskis' invitation to bring our minds as well as our senses into the cinema, the film is awash with clues. Whether verbally or visually, subtle hints point us towards the central themes of the film. An early and well-known example is Neo's practice of hiding his illicit computer discs in a copy of Baudrillard's *Simulacra and Simulation*. This isn't just a film for meatheads; it's a film to stretch the mind, to bring philosophy to the masses. Themes of reality, choice, free will and belief burst out at every twist and turn of the plot. *The Matrix* is a film that rewards serious analysis. It makes intellectual film accessible to people who just want action, and it makes action acceptable for people who want cinema to stimulate the mind. *The Matrix* covers all the bases, drawing in a wide cross-section of film fans and satisfying on a number of different levels.

Guns. Lots of guns

Unusually for such an intellectually satisfying film, there is plenty of violence in *The Matrix*. Not the shocking brutality of *Saving Private Ryan* (1998) or *Reservoir Dogs* (1992), but spectacular and glitzy Hollywood violence. The memorable lobby scene where Neo and Trinity break into an office building to rescue Morpheus from the Agents features a driving techno-

metal soundtrack, balletic movements and a hail of bullets ripping both building and security guards to pieces.
The visual refrain of pillars fragmenting, empty bullet
casings falling to the ground and the casual tossing
away of guns mid-fight all serve to glamorise what
should arguably be a horrific scene. Remember, the
people being shot are not Agents (programs of the system: the enemy) but ordinary unenlightened humans –
the very victims that Neo and the rebels are trying to
liberate from the Matrix. Granted that in the context of
Neo and Trinity's mission, the deaths are necessary and
unavoidable. Granted that Morpheus has previously
warned Neo (and the watching audience) that anyone
still plugged into the Matrix is a potential enemy, vul-
nerable to being taken over by an Agent at any moment.
Nevertheless, this scene could have been played as one
of tragic loss, with Neo and Trinity painfully aware of the
human cost of their actions. Instead it is presented in a
way that encourages the audience to bay for more.
When the British actor Simon Pegg talked about the
scene for Channel 4's *100 Greatest Films*,[26] he commented that when he saw Neo and Trinity just throwing
away their guns, rather than pausing to reload, his reaction was to think 'cool'. And he's right, it was.

Fighting for a purpose

Not that the action scenes are just a spoonful of sugar
to help the red pill go down. Audiences may have been
drawn in by the special effects in the trailers, but the
key action scenes also play a vital part in the development of plot and character. The film's first significant
sequence (after the opening lines of code and the

[26] First broadcast on British television by Channel 4 on 24th November 2001.

telephone trace program) is Trinity's escape from a combination of policemen and Agents. The fight scene where she leaves four policemen crumpled on the floor of room 303 shows that she can handle herself, to say the least. But the final confirmation that her abilities are way beyond normal human parameters comes when first Trinity, and then an Agent make the huge leap from one rooftop to another. The astonished policeman also speaks for the audience when he says 'That's impossible.' This first action sequence of the film is a drawing back of the curtain, the first indication that the world we are watching is not all we might expect it to be.

Similarly, the kung fu scene in the Construct is more than just a chance for Fishburne and Reeves to put their five months of combat training to good use.[27] Morpheus' concern is not with Neo's technique. Rather, he wants to teach him how to think: to learn how to bend or break the laws that govern the Matrix. Morpheus points out to Neo that their speed and strength in the Construct (and therefore in the Matrix itself) do not depend on their muscles in the real world. 'What are you waiting for?' he cries, 'You're faster than this. Don't think you are, know you are. Come on! Stop trying to hit me and hit me!' This virtual fight is all about Neo's mind, his belief in his own ability to manipulate the program, to bend its laws to his own will. And Neo's failure when he first attempts the jump program shows us that he still has a long way to go before he can lead humanity to victory against the machines. For the time being, at least, he quite literally falls short of the standard required.

[27] According to the promotional documentary *Do You Know Kung Fu?* they were expecting combat training to last just two weeks.

Our first glimpse of bullet time (when Neo and Trinity have reached the roof of the building where Morpheus is being held) also demonstrates that Neo is growing in his ability to manipulate the Matrix. Neo dodges a hail of slow motion bullets fired by an Agent. Once the Agent has been dealt with, Trinity asks Neo 'How did you do that? You moved like they do – I've never seen anyone move that fast.' It is apparent that Neo is gaining self-belief, and growing into his calling as the One.

Throughout the film (and most notably in the extended sequence where Neo first confronts Agent Smith in the subway, then runs, dies and finally returns to life with unparalleled power) special effects and action are used to serve the story. These scenes are not present merely to pander to the appetite of an audience desperate for spectacle and sensation. It is quite possible to watch *The Matrix* just for the action, and to be satisfied on that level. Indeed many *Matrix* fans regard the philosophical backdrop as boring pretension, something to be endured while waiting for the next kick-ass fight scene. Nevertheless, this is an action film with much more going for it than just the action set pieces, regardless of how groundbreaking they may be.

Becoming the One

He's starting to believe.
MORPHEUS

At the heart of *The Matrix* is a journey of self-discovery. We first meet Thomas Anderson as a disenchanted outsider. Working for a software company by day[28] and

---

[28] An alternate reality online game, posing as a website for the fictitious company, can be found at www.metacortechs.com

living under the hacker pseudonym of 'Neo' by night. By the end of the film, all of his (and our) preconceptions about the nature of the world around him have been blown away, and Neo has been transformed. He is 'The One', the long awaited saviour of humanity in their long war against the machines. The words of his manager at the software company turn out to have more than a touch of irony:

> You have a problem with authority, Mr Anderson. You believe that you are special. That, somehow the rules do not apply to you. Obviously you are mistaken.

The film tells the story of how Neo discovers that he is not mistaken. He *is* special; the rules *don't* apply to him.

Neo discovers that what he thinks of as the real world is a computer generated illusion, designed to keep him and the rest of humanity enslaved. He is told that humans exist only as batteries, providing energy for the machines whose artificial intelligence is responsible for the design and maintenance of the Matrix. The only hope for humanity lies in the prophecy that one day a saviour will come, a human with the power to control the Matrix, the One.

The journey that Neo makes in the film is inside his head, in more ways than one. Geographically, he doesn't seem to travel very far – the action all taking place in a small area of the city that was very familiar to Neo before Morpheus opened his eyes (eyes that Neo has never used before). As Neo is taken to meet the Oracle, he notices a noodle bar where he used to eat. Even though Neo is on familiar territory, he recognises that everything is different, because he now realises that everything he has known is a lie. Even if Neo had travelled thousands of miles to meet the Oracle and to rescue Morpheus, rather than a few blocks, his journey would still have been one which – quite literally – took place within his head, because that's essentially the only place where his old world exists.

Fighting against fate

From the moment Neo wakes up on the *Nebuchadnezzar*, he is made aware of the expectations that everybody has of him. Crew member after crew member reveal themselves to be excited at the prospect of seeing what Neo can do, but the man himself is unsure. When Neo first meets Morpheus, he tells him that he doesn't believe in fate because he doesn't like the idea that he isn't in control. The weight of expectation placed upon Neo, the sense that the path of his life is running out of his control, makes for a hesitant and unwilling would-be messiah.

When Neo meets the Oracle, his fears are confirmed – he isn't the One. He is wracked with doubts, and she tells him 'being the One is a bit like being in love. No one can tell you you're in love, you just know it, through and through, balls to bone.' Neo doesn't have that absolute belief in himself and his role. When the Oracle infers that he isn't the One – that he's got the gift, but it looks like he's waiting for something – Neo hears what he has been telling himself all along: it's not him. He's just a normal guy. He isn't at the centre of something beyond his control.

We shouldn't be too quick to dismiss the Oracle for apparently getting it wrong with Neo, even without knowing subsequent revelations in the later films. The following exchange between Morpheus and Neo is significant:

Neo: And she knows what – everything?

Morpheus: She would say she knows enough.

Neo: And she's never wrong?

Morpheus: Try not to think of it as right and wrong. She is a guide, Neo, she can help you to find the path.

The Oracle tells Neo precisely what he needed to hear. Although Neo interpreted her as saying that he wasn't the One, what she actually said wasn't so much a 'no' as a 'not yet'. She also gave him the information necessary to send him willingly down the hero's path: she let slip that Neo would have to choose between Morpheus' life and his own. Meanwhile, in the background to the scene, a jazz record is playing. The title of the song in question? *I'm Beginning To See The Light*.[29]

Morpheus is captured by the Agents because his unshakeable belief in Neo's identity made him willing to be captured in order to keep Neo safe. Neo's belief that he is not the One made him determined to rescue Morpheus. Once released from the weight of expectation, Neo becomes free to act, and – without knowing what he is doing – sets his foot back on the path that he is destined for. Earlier in the film, as Neo prepares to attempt the jump program, Morpheus says 'You have to let it all go, Neo – fear, doubt and disbelief. Free your mind.' Neo is only able to do this once the burden of being the One is lifted from him.

Neo: Morpheus believed something. And he was ready to give his life for what he believed – I understand that now. That's why I have to go.

---

[29] *I'm Beginning To See The Light*, written by Duke Ellington, Don George, Johnny Hodges and Harry James. Performed by Duke Ellington (RCA records).

Tank: Why?

Neo: Because I believe in something.

Trinity: What?

Neo: I believe I can bring him back.

'Knowing' that he isn't the One, Neo is able to act self-lessly to save Morpheus' life. Neo's belief that Morpheus is more important than him is crucial to this decision and, with this act of self-sacrifice, he takes up his burden. Many people have commented on the Oracle's guess as to what Neo was waiting for ('Your next life maybe – who knows?') as indication that his resurrection enabled him to assume his position as saviour to humanity. But the signs were there before that. Morpheus recognises that Neo is starting to believe as he watches him rescue Trinity from the crashing helicopter, and this occurs before his death. Similarly, Neo's decision to stand and fight Agent Smith is prior to his death (and let's not forget that Neo seems to win this first encounter, something that we are told nobody else has ever managed to do). It is true that once Trinity's profession of love prompts Neo to rise he demonstrates previously unparalleled authority over the Agents and the Matrix itself, but there is also a strong argument that Neo was firmly on the way to Oneness long before Smith's bullets cut him down.

The hero's path

The influence that Joseph Campbell's *Hero With A Thousand Faces* had on George Lucas' *Star Wars* films is well reported.[30] Campbell argued that all stories draw on a limited well of imagery and symbolism. The

---

[30] See David Wilkinson's *The Power of the Force: The Spirituality of the Star Wars films* (Lion Publishing, 2000), p.72-75, for example.

effect of this is that all heroic tales are essentially a retelling of the same story – a story Campbell described as the monomyth. Campbell identified a recurring pattern that can be detected in great heroic tales from a wide range of cultures, ages and belief systems. A pattern occurs again and again: separation, initiation and the acquisition of new powers, and finally returning to the community in order to protect and preserve it. The would-be hero is always an Everyman figure, called to the path of the hero either by chance or by deliberate choice. In Neo's case, there is something of both – he has been searching for Morpheus, but at the same time he has no idea of the role that fate has marked out for him.[31]

Other key elements identified by Campbell can be interpreted as being present in *The Matrix*. To take just a few examples: Neo's loss of nerve in his first window-ledge escape from the Agents can be seen as the initial refusal of the call, as can Neo's early conclusion that Morpheus has got it all wrong, that he isn't the One; Morpheus fills the role of the father-figure mentor; even the moment where a resurrected Neo dives inside Agent Smith echoes the common motif of the hero wearing the skin of an enemy. Finally, like all good heroes, Neo is transformed and equipped with the extraordinary powers required to protect his people.[32] The film ends with

---

[31] Christian commentators have also observed the recurring motifs in the myths and legends of ancient peoples. Writers such as C. S. Lewis and J. R. R. Tolkien regarded the heart of the Christian story as being the myth which was also a fact, with all other manifestations of the monomyth being pale imitations which nevertheless point the way to the truest form of the story. For more on this see Brian Godawa, *Hollywood Worldviews – Watching Films with Wisdom and Discernment* (InterVarsity Press, 2002), p.25-34.

[32] For more detailed analysis of the correspondence of both *The Matrix* and *Star Wars* to Campbell's pattern, see http://www.jitterbug.com/origins/myth.html

victory against the machines seemingly assured, and Neo's path seems to have come full circle. Of course, there were two more films to come, and Neo's triumph against the system proves to be premature, but we didn't know that back in 1999.

The postmodern myth

It can be argued that one of the reasons that *The Matrix* stuck such a chord with its audience was that the Wachowskis had tapped into classic heroic arche-type, drawing on the enduring staples of mythology to retell the monomyth, the hero's story, for a new generation. That they combined it with a multi-layered account of postmodern philosophical themes makes their achievement all the more remarkable.

And what a retelling they gave us. The nature of the monomyth, according to Campbell, is that each culture takes the essential pattern of the story and uses it to air its own concerns. The Wachowskis mix together a heady cocktail of themes: reality and illusion; free will and destiny; man and machine. Larry Wachowski has commented on how the brothers' love for action films was tempered with a sense of frustration at how hollow many of those films were. 'We were determined to put as many ideas into the movie as we could.'[33]

With the extraordinary attention to detail that went into *The Matrix*, it is reasonable to assume that the decision to set the film (or at least, the virtual world featured in the film) in the then contemporary world of 1999 was taken for reasons beyond the convenience of finding locations.

---

[33] Christopher Probst, 'Welcome to the Machine', *American Cinematographer*, 80.4 (April 1999), p.32.

Underpinning the post-apocalyptic future and the war between men and machines, underpinning Neo's heroics and Cypher's treachery lies a question (one which should drive us?): what difference does it make to me? Unless the Wachowskis really are trying to convince us that someone has literally pulled a virtual dreamworld over our eyes, what meaning should we draw from *The Matrix*? When Agent Smith is interrogating Morpheus he makes this comment:

> Have you ever stood and stared at it, marvelled at its beauty, its genius? Billions of people just living out their lives, oblivious.

And of course, those billions of people are the reason why Morpheus, Neo and the others are risking their lives hacking into the Matrix. They want others to break free, to be able to live their lives without falling under the influence of external control.

Cypher knows the truth – he knows that life plugged into the Matrix is an illusion; he knows that only outside is there any true life and freedom for him. And yet he chooses to go back. He is willing to hand over his commanding officer, to sell out everyone living in Zion and to cold-bloodedly kill his friends. And what is it that he wants? Comfortable illusion.[34]

> I know this steak doesn't exist. I know that when I put it in my mouth the Matrix is telling my brain that it is juicy and delicious. After nine years you know what I've realised? Ignorance is bliss.

Cypher wants out of real life, because it's too hard. He opts for an easier life – the life where he doesn't ques-

---

[34] Cypher's name within the Matrix was Mr Reagan, which makes his request to be 'rich, someone important – like an actor' and his demand not to remember anything, sound worryingly similar to another Mr Reagan that you may be able to think of.

tion, where he doesn't have to think. A life much like the cosseted, commercialised world of the late twentieth/early twenty-first century, where multinational corporations dictate what we wear, what we eat and even to some extent what we think tastes good.

Read Mercer Schuchardt[35] suggests that the film is riddled with hints that the Matrix represents our own modern day world. From Agent Smith's account of Thomas Anderson's 'normal' life (working for a large corporation, possessing a social security number, paying his taxes) to Morpheus' account of the Matrix's presence when Neo watches TV, when he goes to work, when he goes to church, the film points us back to our own experience. Schuchardt suggests that these clues point to the things in our own lives that form a means of control. Is *The Matrix* a clarion call to independence? A counter-cultural blast against going with the corporate flow? Should we follow Neo's example and struggle to free our own minds?

Many perspectives on the One

There are many different views as to what *The Matrix* is all about. In addition to Schuchardt's analysis, the film can be read as an allegory of Christian belief (with Neo as a Christ figure, a saviour who rises from the dead to deliver humanity from slavery and hopelessness). Equally, it can be seen as a Buddhist parable (this world is an illusion, and life is a journey to enlightenment). In some Islamic countries, the films were even kept from the cinemas because they were seen as Zionist propaganda. Many groups were quick to see

[35] Read Mercer Schuchardt, 'What is the Matrix?' in *Take The Red Pill*, Glenn Yeffeth (ed.) (Summersdale, 2003) p.10-30.

something of their own story in *The Matrix*, and although the Wachowskis are happy to pick and mix elements of different mythologies and religions in order to tell their tale, at no point have they given any indication of endorsing any such interpretation. A clearer picture of the Wachowskis intention would emerge with the subsequent films in the trilogy, but even when all we had to go on was the first film, *The Matrix* always seemed to be more concerned with arguing philosophical points than it was about promoting the truth claims of any particular religion.

What is certain is that *The Matrix* seems to present us with a definitive and final victory. The closing sequence shows Neo talking on the phone, presumably addressing the Agents or some other representative of the Matrix:

> I'm going to show these people what you don't
> want them to see. I'm going to show them a world
> without you. A world without rules and controls,
> without borders and boundaries. A world where
> anything is possible. Where we go from there is a
> choice I leave with you.

Why does Neo leave this choice up to the machines? Perhaps because after everything that we have seen him do, it is unthinkable that the machines would be able to stop him. Neo and the audience end the film secure in the knowledge that the victory against the machines has been won. Or at least, that's what we thought.

CHAPTER 3

Everything you know is wrong: *The Matrix Reloaded*

by Clive Thorne

I have dreamed a dream, but now that dream is gone from me.

Sequels are tricky. It is too easy to fall into the trap of revamping an established plot line with already filled-out characters and just produce a reworking of the original story. A sequel is only going to be considered for a successful film and so the temptation may be to leave a winning formula alone and produce a cinematic clone (witness the *Batman* movies, the *Police Academy* series, the various *Nightmares on Elm Street* and the seemingly endless James Bond franchise). A film that manages to rise above and even better the original is quite a rare phenomenon. The second instalment in a trilogy suffers from the further hurdle of being in the middle. It lacks both the novelty of introducing characters, setting and plot that the first film enjoys, and also misses the dramatic climax of the story that is the prerogative of the third film. There is a need to avoid the impression that this is just a delay in getting to the real action of the final chapter.

To be successful, the second film needs to deepen our grasp of established characters, introduce some new faces, effects and plot twists, and generally take the storyline to a new level. As the middle chapter, it would be best to end with a massive, cliff-hanging setback which keeps the audience in suspense ready for the final resolution of the story – *The Empire Strikes Back* (1980) (widely reckoned to be the best of the original *Star Wars* trilogy) does this and so, happily, does *The Matrix Reloaded*. It seems to me to be an entirely worthy sequel to the original. Not everyone would agree, however, and several critics expressed disappointment with the film.

New faces, new effects

The most significant of the newcomers seem to be the white-bearded Architect, who designs and maintains the Matrix; the single-purpose Keymaker; seemingly independent programs like ze oh-so French Merovingian and his disenchanted wife Persephone; as well as redundant designs like Werewolves and the Banshee-like twins in the service of the Merovingian's underground kingdom. Of the characters from the first film, the Oracle is first revealed to be a sentient program and later implied to be the co-designer or 'mother of the Matrix'. Agent Smith is developed as a rogue, self-replicating program no longer working for the system but operating to a new agenda, intent on grabbing power for his own ends. Most surprisingly, Neo turns out to be not so much the One, as the latest One – an anomaly within the Matrix that the Architect had been expecting, and whose function is not to destroy the Matrix but to ensure its continuation.

The special effects build on the groundbreaking success of the John Gaetta's work in the first film and the freeway car chase must rank as the most spectacular (and possibly the longest) in cinematic history. The breathtaking sight of an Agent crushing a moving car as he uses it as a stepping-stone was widely – and effectively – used in the previews to the film. However, the sequence of state-of-the-art special effects when Neo fights multiple copies of Agent Smith, although technically accomplished, has been seen by some as unnecessary, overlong and bordering on the ridiculous. Some critics have observed a change in the use of special effects and action between the first two films in the trilogy. In *The Matrix* these served to advance the plot and reveal character.[36] In *The Matrix Reloaded*, however, the action is arguably less tied in to developing the story and seems more concerned with throwing in another fight to keep the audience interested. Neo's now-realised powers mean that his fights lack suspense, and at times (as with the encounter with an ever growing army of Smiths) descend into the comic.

We get to see the human city of Zion and learn of its power structure (Morpheus, it seems, has less authority than we previously assumed) and imminent danger from the army of digging Sentinel machines (first introduced in the *Animatrix* short film *The Final Flight of the Osiris* (2003)). The organic 'humanness' of the city is emphasised by its pervading dirty environment and a sweatily orgiastic celebration of sensual ecstasy in the Temple – quite a contrast to the antiseptically clean surroundings of the Architect's inner sanctum. The defiant outpouring of animal emotion in Zion is diametrically opposed to the cold, clinical, machine-like delivery of the Architect's speech (which drew a yawn from a near-

---

[36] See previous chapter for examples from *The Matrix*.

by member of the audience when I first watched it). Neo's messianic, almost god-like role is also reinforced by the veneration and awe that he inspires from the masses in Zion.

The wool pulled over your eyes

The relationship between the real world and the virtual world of the Matrix becomes a major twist in the plot. Agent Smith manages to download his programmed will into Bane, one of the Zion rebels, who then acts under his direction – even to the extent of a hastily aborted attempt to kill Neo. Neo has real world dreams foreseeing the exact circumstances of Trinity's death, events that are later confirmed by the Architect to be part of the Matrix, designed to present Neo with a choice. Yet Trinity's presence in the Matrix at the time of her death was prompted by an attack in the real world, which knocked out one of the ships leading her to make a choice, again in the real world, to reverse her previous decision to remain outside of the Matrix. How can the Architect anticipate this in the prepared choice he offers to Neo about intervening to save Trinity and how is Neo able to dream about it so accurately before any of it happens? Does the Architect have absolute control over certain events in the real world, including characters' actions and decisions? If things had turned out differently, would he simply have reprogrammed a different choice for Neo? Is some sort of mythic, mystical premonition by Neo implied in his dream? By the end of the film, we are led specifically towards the possibility that the 'real world' is another layer of the Matrix program when Neo incapacitates some Sentinels merely by holding up his hand against them. However, by the time the credits roll at the end of the film, everything is left up in the air – we know that many of the assumptions we made about the world of the first film have been blown out of the water, but we don't yet know what to put in their place. The audience is left trying to figure out for themselves what is really happening. This may be a good strategy for encouraging people to see the film more than once and for building suspense and anticipation for the third instalment, but it also led to a sense of frustration for many cinema-goers, eager to know what is really going on.

Just another system of control

The theme of control and purpose seems to dominate *The Matrix Reloaded*. On meeting Neo, Agent Smith says, 'Here we both are, apparently free ... but not free' and goes on to say that the only meaning is found in purpose. Neo says to the Oracle, 'If you already know, how can I make a choice?' and she says, 'You have already made the choice, now you have to understand it.' The Keymaker tells an Agent trying to capture him, 'We do only what we are meant to do.' When asked how he knows details of the Architect's building he says, 'I know because I must know, it is my purpose.' He subsequently accepts his death as something that was meant to be because his purpose had been fulfilled. The clearest statement of this theme comes from the Merovingian who explains at length that freedom and choice do not exist, with cause and effect reigning supreme as the determining factor for everything that anyone does. He illustrates his point with a demonstration of chemical control over the actions of a female character in the Matrix. He says that power comes from understanding the nature of this causality and using it ... 'choice is an illusion, created between those with power and those without.'[37]

The final demonstration of control comes in the interview with the Architect who refers to Neo as 'the eventuality of an anomaly' designed to deal with flaws in the system of the Matrix. We learn that there have been previous editions of 'the One' and that the whole business of the prophecy of the One is simply a device to control the destruction and rebirth of Zion, which has occurred five times before. Zion itself is said also to be a device to deal with the need for the human mind to have an illusion of free will and choice. The original design of the Matrix, as we discovered in the previous film, was a complete human paradise in absolute harmony but the human mind would not accept or believe it and the system failed. A reworking including the brutality, violence and suffering of the human experience also crashed because it excluded choice. It was the intuitive program of the Oracle that discovered a way of maintaining a stable Matrix system through the prophecy of the One and the illusion of free action in Zion. But the uncontrolled growth of Zion would also lead to instability in the system and so it has to be periodically destroyed and restarted. This, it seems, is the function and purpose of the One.

The control of Neo by the Matrix system is emphasised by the ranks of TV monitors around him that all show his image reacting in different ways in other simulations. Now and then the camera focuses on one of the screens and then it resolves from there onto the 'real' Neo, showing us again and again how he is anticipated

[37] For a fuller examination of this theme in the films, see chapter 9.

by the system. The Architect is even able to predict Neo's choice of a first question. This revelation has a lot of implications for what we have already seen in the first two films. It implies that the whole prophecy belief system so dear to Morpheus is a lie (which Neo points out once he is back on the *Nebuchadnezzar*) and that there is no certainty in the prediction of a defeat of the machines by Neo. It suggests that all the exciting fight scenes, with their split-second reactions and narrowest of escapes, are all minutely expected and their outcomes anticipated by the Architect. For example, Neo only rescues Morpheus and the Keymaker from Agents of the Matrix system in the freeway explosion by an amazing last second fly-past. But the Keymaker has an essential part to play in getting Neo to his preordained interview with the Architect, so to what extent was he ever in any real danger? This might help to explain how our intrepid heroes continually manage to evade hails of bullets! It even throws up the possibility that Trinity and Neo's love for one another may also be a design of the system (although it is hinted that this love is a new element in this sixth running of the Matrix program). In *The Matrix*, Trinity's love for Neo is predicted by the Oracle and is crucial in the real world for the revival of Neo from the dead and therefore the whole continuing program for the destruction of Zion and the resetting of the Matrix. At the end of *Reloaded*, we are left wondering just how much is under the direct control of the Matrix. Do our heroes have any real freedom of choice, or are they – as the Merovingian argues – merely victims of causality? There is the overall impression of rats being put through an experimental maze.

The problem is choice

When he is with the Architect, Neo says 'the problem is choice' and choice features at the climax of both *The Matrix* and *The Matrix Reloaded*. It seems that the whole storyline in both films leads up to presenting Neo with a choice. In *The Matrix*, the Oracle tells Neo that he will have to make a choice between himself and Morpheus, choosing whether to risk his own life in order to save Morpheus from the Agents. This is made harder by the Oracle's prediction that either he or Morpheus will die. In *Reloaded*, the Architect uses two doors to symbolise Neo's choice, and the stakes are raised as he has to choose between saving the Matrix system and letting his beloved Trinity die, or trying to save Trinity and risking the death of all humanity with the catastrophic collapse of the Matrix and the destruction of Zion. Again the Architect says that he cannot save Trinity. The first choice is about self-preservation versus loyalty and love for friends, and Neo chooses to risk his life to try to save Morpheus. Neo does indeed die, but is then revived by Trinity. The second choice is much starker as it is basically between his lover's life and the risk of the destruction of all humanity including himself. Neo again chooses to risk everything for the sake of love. What is the meaning of these choices?

Some saw a possible clue in *Matriculated* (2003), the last short film of *The Animatrix*. In this animation, a fighting machine is captured by a group of humans who hope to convert it to fighting on their side through re-educating it using an artificial virtual environment to give it a choice to embrace new values. The system presents Neo with choices. His decision to save Morpheus is followed by a sort of rebirth and an increase in his powers to a new level of control over the Matrix and its Agents and his decision to save Trinity is followed by successfully bringing her back to life and then demonstrating a new level of control over the real world Sentinels. He gets more power each time that he chooses love over himself or the system. After *The Matrix Reloaded* came out, there was a theory on some of the Internet discussion boards that Neo would turn out to be a captured machine that is being re-educated by humans through the virtual reality of the Matrix to be offered choices to value friendship, love and self-sacrifice and so to convert to their side.

Whatever the motivation, the climactic choices that conclude both *The Matrix* and *The Matrix Reloaded* remain crucial to the plot of their respective films. Unravelling the meaning behind them will lead us nearer to the underlying message of the trilogy. Is it about the almost mystical power of love to overcome even the most seemingly omnipotent oppression? Or the strength of the individual against the system? Or human free will and creativity triumphing over the programmed responses of machines? Or the need for humans and machines to live together in some kind of harmonious symbiotic relationship? Or some combination of these? Or even something else altogether?

It's a machine's world

The idea of the interdependence of humans and machines is in the basic context of the plot of *The Matrix Reloaded*, in contrast to the more malevolent picture of the machine intelligences in the first film. A hint of this may be found when the Oracle says, 'I'm interested in one thing: the future. And believe me, I know, the only way to get there is together' – co-opera-tion between machines and humans. Machines grow humans like a crop because their bodies provide the electrical power that the machines need in order to function. The humans are tended and physically cared for by the machines, who also provide a suitable mental environment in which their minds can flourish. The fact that the machines tried to provide a harmonious human paradise as the first Matrix environment suggests a lack of vindictiveness on their part and after their solar power supply was cut off they seem to be motivated by a pragmatic need to survive rather than something more sinister.

The extent to which humans have needed machines to survive has increased as technology has advanced. Councillor Hamann points this out to Neo when they visit the engineering level of Zion. He asks Neo what is the difference between the control exercised by the machines in the engineering level and the ones running the Matrix. In one case control is via an artificial reali-ty, in the other it is by way of supplying vital air, water and food. Neo says that the difference is that they could turn the machines in Zion off, but the Councillor ques-tions whether that is the actually the case – to switch off the machines would mean the end of life in Zion. Where does co-operation end and control begin? There is also the question of whether the controlled environment provided by the Matrix could be preferable to the hard-ships of the real world. Do the comforts that machines provide us with enslave us to continuing to maintain them?

The whole human versus machine debate is becom-ing ever more relevant as our technology advances and machines invade more and more areas of our lives. They have begun to invade our bodies with simple pace-makers and work progresses fast to produce everything from prosthetic eyes to chips that can be implanted in the brain to help control neural illnesses through the release of drugs or electrical stimulation. See how dependent the average teenager is on their mobile phone, or how many hours we spend wedded to computers and drinking in the life-giving flow of the Internet. We don't have to look too far for a ready-made vision of a future that is just around the corner. A teenager without a mobile phone can feel like a social outcast; and how many of us could manage without our computers even now? How long before the machines invade our minds in some form of virtual reality? Will this threaten to control us or just be a further development in humanity's increasingly interdependent relationship with his creations? Councillor Hamann's point seems to be becoming truer each day in our real world.

The Matrix Reloaded is a sequel that builds on the success of the first film, expanding the horizons of the characters and the plot and introducing questions about the extent to which people are truly autonomous or free to make their own choices, which it intriguingly leaves hard to pin down. The film finishes with the suspense of the unresolved threat to Zion, and the fact that the only survivor of the battle is the Smith-controlled Bane points to the further role that character will play in the final outcome of the conflict. Will Neo have to face off against Agent Smith yet again, but this time with the stakes being the control of the Matrix system? Or will the Architect prove to have been in absolute control all along? At the end of *Reloaded* many such questions remain, but with the so-called prophecy exposed as a design of the system, there is no longer any sense of certainty that Neo can save the day, and we were left to eagerly anticipate a resolution in the third film.

CHAPTER 4

It ends tonight:
The Matrix Revolutions

by Steve Couch

Everything that has a beginning has an end.

So what was that all about then? The trilogy may have
been brought to a conclusion, but not necessarily one
that all the fans were happy about. Queuing to see the
film a second time, I overheard some teenage girls dis-
cussing their expectations. One of them told the others,
'I'll kill them if it doesn't have a happy ending.' It's
debatable whether or not the Wachowskis can sleep
safely in their beds – is the ending a happy one or not?
The war is over, which is good. But the Matrix still
exists, with lots of people still plugged in, which is bad.
But the Architect says whoever wants to be free will be
released, which is good. But Neo is dead, which is very
bad. But the Oracle says that she suspects we'll see him
again one day, which is ... keeping the options open for
a possible sequel. Loose ends of the story are tied up,
although some are left ambiguously flapping in the
computer generated breeze. It wasn't the ending some
fans were hoping for, but maybe you can't see past the
denouement you don't understand.

Producer Joel Silver has described *The Matrix
Reloaded* and *The Matrix Revolutions* as being like

two halves of the same movie,[38] and to a large extent *Revolutions* carries on where its predecessor left off. We see the crew of the wrecked *Nebuchadnezzar* on board another ship, the *Hammer*, but Neo is still in a coma after stopping the Sentinels in their tracks at the end of *Reloaded*. Much of what follows fits the expectations we might have had after *Reloaded*, but there are also significant developments to direct our thinking in a new way. As Morpheus and Niobe might have it, some things in this trilogy never change, but some things do.

A changed man

One significant change, which adds to the dramatic tension during the action scenes, is that it is quickly established that Neo is not all-powerful. The laid-back, almost bored facial expression that characterised his fight with the Agents at the beginning of *Reloaded* is wiped off Keanu's face by his adventures in Mobil Ave train station. As he postures and threatens to get the Trainman to let him return to the Matrix with Sati and her family, he (aptly enough, given his location) gets nowhere. When the Trainman explains that 'down here I make the rules. Down here I make the threats. Down here I'm God', the Wachowskis make it clear that Neo's superpowers aren't always enough. Later, when Smith hovers in the sky and claims 'This is my world! My world!', the echo of the earlier scene is enough to make us doubt whether Neo has got what it takes to successfully slug it out. Meanwhile, back in limbo, Neo decides that as the strong-arm stuff hasn't worked, he'll rely on his ability to travel large distances to get out of trouble. But following the train down the tunnel only brings him

[38] *Empire* magazine, December 2003, p.94.

right back where he started. Where before we saw Neo speed hundreds of miles to rescue his friends, now he can't even make it more than a hundred yards and is dependent on others to rescue him. Although Neo's superpowers are still intact, he can't always rely on them to save the day. The message is clear: even the One can't be too sure of himself anymore. And the film is all the stronger for it.

But Neo's powers are still a formidable force, and they have grown. As revealed at the end of *Reloaded*, they somehow now function in the real world. It is unclear whether the real world is real, or whether it is just another layer of the Matrix,[39] but if the former is true, how come Neo gets to be the One even when he's not plugged in? Early clues are given in his neural activity while comatose on the *Hammer*. For some reason, his mind seems to still be located in the Matrix, even though his body isn't connected. When Morpheus and Trinity are bringing Neo back after his rescue from the train station, Link doesn't recognise Neo's coding – something is different about Neo. Later the Oracle explains that the power of the One extends beyond the world of the Matrix because of his connection to the Source. It is never (I think) made entirely clear how this works, but the end result is that Neo's perception of the real world is radically altered. When Neo is blinded in his fight with Bane, not only does his new-found vision

[39] This is the subject of heated online debate. After a first viewing of *Revolutions* I took the view that Zion and the real world was real. I am now becoming persuaded of the opposite view. A number of small details across all three films – (for example, the fact that during their final fight Neo and Smith crash through a wall into the kung fu room from *The Matrix* – a room located in the Construct on the *Nebuchadnezzar*, rather than the Matrix itself) suggest that the Wachowskis, typically, have decided to hint and leave a trail of clues rather than provide a clear answer.

get him out of trouble, but it also proves superior – the golden image that he sees reveals Bane's true form – unlike the man on the hovercraft, the man in the flame is wearing glasses. Like the blind seers of Greek mythology Neo doesn't miss his sight, because what has taken its place helps him to see more clearly. And finally, for the first time in the trilogy, Neo understands what he has to do.

A dark power rises

Neo isn't the only one with new powers to play with. As Neo has grown in stature throughout the trilogy, so too has his nemesis, Agent Smith. As the Oracle puts it to Neo:

> He is you, your opposite, your negative. The result of the equation trying to balance itself out.

But just as Neo found it hard getting used to the idea that little old Thomas Anderson was actually the saviour of the world (well may you 'whoa', Mr Anderson), so Smith doesn't find the accumulation of new selves entirely straightforward. Bane's self-inflicted wounds give some indication of mental disturbance (understandable in the circumstances – Bane later comments to Neo that 'it is difficult to think encased in this rotting meat, the stink of it filling every breath'), and when the Matrix-bound Smith has successfully assimilated the Oracle, his first reaction is to take off his dark glasses, look around and then let out the most maniacal evil laugh heard this side of a pantomime villain. Just as Neo has been on a journey of self-discovery, so his counterpart has travelled away from a place called sanity, and now appears to be seriously unhinged.

But if Neo is to be the saviour of the world, so Smith must take on a balancing role, as the Oracle explains:

Everything that has a beginning has an end. I see
the end coming. I see the darkness spreading. I
see death, and you are all that stands in his way.
Death is a he rather than an it, and Neo instantly realises who the Oracle means. The clothes may be sharper,
but the Grim Reaper is still clad in black. The purpose
of life, he tells Neo, is to end, and it looks like he intends
to help everyone to fulfil their purpose.

The puppet-mistress

'Some things in this world stay the same, and some
things change.' And some manage to do both at the
same time. The Oracle is (enforced change of actress
notwithstanding) arguably the most consistent and
unchanging character throughout the trilogy. What has
changed dramatically with every film is our understanding of who and what she actually is.

In *The Matrix*, the Oracle is a wise guide to the
humans, telling them what they need to know in order
to fight the machines. She is an old, respected standard
bearer of the rebellion. By the end of *Reloaded*, not
only has it been revealed that she is a program, but it is
implied that she played a significant role in shaping the
Matrix in its current form, earning the title of 'mother
of the Matrix'. As a result, Neo and the others begin to
doubt whether or not her guidance can be trusted – is
she just another system of control, manipulating their
decisions and usurping their free will?

The Matrix Revolutions reveals the Oracle to be perhaps the most significant character of the whole trilogy.
Although the dramatic focus is on Neo, and as the One
he carries the burden of ending the war, it is the Oracle
who has plotted and schemed to bring the plan to

fruition. Where we thought we were watching a battle between man and machine, between Neo and Smith, Zion and the Sentinels, the central conflict of the films turns out to be between the Oracle and the Architect. Just as Neo and Smith are in balanced opposition to one another, so too are the two powerful programs. His purpose is to balance the equation, hers to unbalance it.

Endgame

At the end of *Revolutions*, the Architect tells the Oracle that she has played a dangerous game, and it is clear that her 'game' has been costly, for her as well as for others. The Oracle's change of appearance is vaguely explained as being a consequence of her meddling in the affairs of the Merovingian. Although it does not appear that a new actress was the Wachowski brothers' original intention for *The Matrix Revolutions*, it was always part of the Oracle's lot to suffer for the cause. When Smith turns up mob-handed at her apartment, he rages at her and speculates as to why she is still there. She undoubtedly knew he was coming, so it must be a deliberate choice to wait for him. Smith's fury is for our benefit – to highlight the fact that the Oracle has chosen to be assimilated, even though by doing so she will make the last enemy more powerful than ever before. She meant it when she told Neo that she was prepared to go just as far as he was. She too was prepared to face death.

Once Smith has the Oracle's foresight, he knows that he will win the climactic battle with Neo. That's why all the other Smiths simply stand and watch – they know that the most powerful of their number, the Smith who was the Oracle, has got what it takes to win the day.

Smith's moment of victory reveals why the Oracle was so willing to fall for the cause:

> Wait, I've seen this! This is it, this is the end.
> I stand right here, and I'm supposed to say
> something. I say, I say ... Everything that has a
> beginning has an end, Neo ... What? What did I
> just say?

At the last, the Oracle proves to be too powerful a program even for Smith to keep under wraps. When Smith uses the name 'Neo' rather than 'Mr Anderson' (Smith alone has consistently used Neo's old name throughout all three films), it becomes obvious that somebody else is doing the talking. Neo realises that it's time to stop fighting and let the final stage of the plan be carried out. But why didn't Smith, with the Oracle's foresight, know that his victory over Neo would be short-lived? The Oracle's much-repeated saying, that we can't see past the choices we don't understand, is perhaps the answer. We have already seen that Agent Smith couldn't understand why the Oracle was waiting for him, and his baiting of Neo throughout their final encounter makes it clear that he has no understanding of Neo's motives, either for fighting or for ceasing to resist. When the Architect talks about the Oracle's 'dangerous game', is he referring simply to the possibility of her failing to manipulate Neo and the others to her ends? Or could he have meant a possibility that the Oracle's power would prove insufficient to keep the sting in the tail hidden from Smith after her assimilation.

The peaceful revolution

Both Smith and the Oracle tell Neo that they want the same thing that he wants, yet there is still a lot of fighting to be done. Everybody seems to want the war to be over, but there isn't a lot of agreement on how it should end. Many fans were expecting a triumph of the humans over the machines, and the end of the Matrix altogether. But within the film there seem to be at least three different approaches to resolving the conflict.

The first view, held by the majority of humans and machines (and, it would seem, disappointed reviewers) was to expect a decisive victory for one side or the other. Either Zion would hold and Neo would strike to inflict a crushing defeat upon the machines, or the free humans would be wiped out trying.[40] This point of view is well encapsulated by Mifune's rabble-rousing speech to his APU corps:

> If it's our time to die, it's our time. All I ask is if
> we have to give these bastards our lives, we give
> them hell before we do.

This sense of hatred is echoed by Smith, who pursues a second way of ending the war. He seems to hate everything, human and machine alike, and for him the end of the war means not the end of one side or the other, but of both. It is made clear that he wouldn't be satisfied with assimilating everyone within the Matrix. Soon Smith will turn his attention to the Machine City itself. Having settled into his new role as Death, Smith seems determined to make a really thorough job of it.

And the existence of a loose cannon like Smith enables Neo to enact the Oracle's plan for a third way – peace between Zion and the Machine City. Does it say

---

[40] Why do the machines need the war to end? Because since the events of *The Matrix*, Zion has been freeing an ever-increasing number of people, and dangerously unbalancing the system, as we learned in *The Matrix Reloaded*.

something for the times in which we live that many viewers were disappointed with this as an outcome? The solution of a peaceful settlement between age-old enemies is somehow seen as a let down, rather than an encouragement to our leaders – and us – to find ways of settling differences, to establish common cause rather than slugging it out to the bitter end.

The Oracle comments that change is always dangerous. The title of the film gives a clue that a simple military victory for one side or the other would never be enough. This is a film about revolutions plural, rather than revolution singular, and the Wachowskis' final solution offers more than a mere military victory. The Oracle is, and always has been, working towards something much wider-ranging, revolutionising the lives of everybody – human or program – living on earth or in the Matrix. In *Reloaded* we discovered the existence of an underground of programs who have outlived their purpose, and in *Revolutions* we are reminded that programs with no purpose, like Sati, must be deleted. When the Oracle asks the Architect about the fate of 'the ones who want out', it is arguable that she is just as concerned with programs as with humans. Hence, at the close of the film the focus is not on the survivors of the siege of Zion, but on programs who have been restored to the Matrix – the Oracle, Sati and Seraph. After the destruction of the Smiths, we see the Oracle lying on the ground where the champion of Smiths fell – all the programs he assimilated have been reinstated and now, thanks to the Oracle's actions, they can compute in safety. This second revolution has been gathering pace throughout the trilogy, even if most of us were unaware of it until the end.

Mecha-Messiah

It isn't clear how Neo effects his final triumph over Smith, bringing in the new age of harmony not only between man and machine, but for inter-machine relations too. Some would argue that Neo is able to shatter all the Smiths simply through the power of the One; others that because Neo and Smith are balanced opposites, when Smith destroys Neo, he also destroys himself. What is clear is that the machines need Neo to deal with the growing problem of Agent Smith. After Neo has been fully assimilated, the scene cuts briefly back to Neo's body in the Machine City. There is a movement of the leads connecting Neo, and a surge of light that seems to suggest something flowing from the machine world and into Neo, rather than the other way round. Whether it is Neo (drawing power from the source) or the machines (downloading something into Neo) that takes the initiative at this moment is open to interpretation. What is clear is that one way or another Neo has become a messiah for the machines as well as for humanity.

There is symbolism to back up this new depth to Neo's prophesied role. It can be argued that, as a human, Neo represents the creator of the machines, as it was the humans who 'gave birth to AI'.[41] When Smith assimilates Neo, Neo becomes another Smith, and therefore can now be considered to be machine as much as human. So the creator takes on the form of his creation. When he then dies in order to ensure the safety of the Machine City, saving all the machines and programs from destruction, the Christian parallels are

[41] As Morpheus told us way back in *The Matrix*.

reinforced further. We see Neo, back in the Machine City, spread-eagled in classic crucifixion pose. More than this, the parallel with Jesus is completed as the body is taken away. Where Jesus' body was taken away for burial by his followers and friends,[42] the faithful who bear Neo's body away are all machines. In each case, the messiah is carried away by those whose salvation he has ensured.

Will the real good guys please stand up?

The question of good and evil is a tricky one to answer. All along we've been expecting the triumph of good (the humans) over evil (the machines). But a viewing of *The Animatrix* gives us pause to consider whether we've got the labels the right way round. Way back in the Matrix pre-history that is told in *The Second Renaissance Parts I and II*, it seems that the machines only wanted to peacefully co-exist, and it was the humans who were set on a master-slave relationship or nothing at all. By allowing the two sides to join forces at the last, perhaps the Wachowskis are questioning whether things are ever quite as simple as the terms good and evil suggest. The ultimate enemy in the films turns out to be Smith, who we have already said takes the role of death – an inevitable force of nature, rather than one of moral evil.

Matrix revelations

We came to the cinema expecting answers. Do we get any? It seems that the message of the film is that belief is a good thing, and knowing yourself is more important than the details of what you put that belief in. When

[42] Luke 23:50-56.

Morpheus, Niobe and Roland are explaining their actions to the Zion Council, Morpheus defends Neo:

> Neo is doing what he believes he must do. I don't know if what he is doing is right ... but I do know that as long as there's a single breath in his body he won't give up. And neither must we.

Neo's single-minded assurance of the path he follows is, it seems, its own justification. Morpheus recognises that we lack the necessary information to know what is the right thing to do, but affirms his friend's actions. Choice is everything.

The films are perhaps about how we face the trials of life and the prospect of death. Even before Neo acquiesces to Smith in order to destroy him, Trinity shows that death is not to be feared. Although both Neo and Trinity have snatched each other back from beyond the jaws of death before, this time it's for keeps, and Trinity is content with that. She tells Neo that she has done all that she can do and that it is time for her to die. Her dying moments, before kissing Neo for the last time, give her a chance to explain why she can be so content at the last:

> I wished I had one more chance to say what really mattered, to say I love you ... to say how grateful I was for every moment I was with you.

Trinity's life is not wasted, because of the love that Neo brought into it, because of the feelings and experiences that Neo and Trinity shared. Smith describes human existence as being without meaning or purpose, but the emotional weight of the film suggests that, as with just about everything that Smith says, we are not necessarily meant to agree with him. Neo's assertion of his choice to keep on fighting presents the thought at the heart of the trilogy: it's all about choice. Like the Existentialists of the twentieth century, the films assert that we give meaning to our lives by the choices that we make. If our choices lead to lives full of love and experience, if we have discovered ourselves and made the choice to grasp life and live it for all it is worth, that is purpose enough. In a world where we cannot be sure of anything – real or illusion, man or machine, victory or defeat – it is enough to know ourselves.

The Matrix Revolutions has been criticised for failing to answer the questions that were posed in the previous films. I think that the film does offer answers of a kind, but not necessarily the ones that everyone was hoping for. There is a world of difference between offering answers that we may find intellectually unsatisfying and offering no answers at all. Many of the loose ends of the films are left for us to tie together, but most if not all can be reconciled with a little thought. And if we still feel hard done by that all our questions aren't settled after a single viewing of the film, maybe we should remember that we were promised *The Matrix Revolutions*, not *The Matrix Resolutions*.

CHAPTER 5

Everything that you don't have to do: The cultural impact of the *Matrix* trilogy

by Steve Tilley

The Matrix has you

What is culture? There are many definitions, some philosophical, some pseudo-scientific, some scarily, genuinely scientific. Perhaps the simplest is from music producer Brian Eno who sees culture as 'everything you don't have to do.'[43] Thus he would say that clothing (in the West) is not culture but fashion is; eating is not culture but cuisine is and so on. On these terms the cultural question about anything is, 'What has this started us doing that we didn't have to do?'

Enter the word string 'Matrix movie' into a search engine such as Google and in one tenth of a second there are one and a half million possible sites to visit, mainly selling wrap-around sunglasses or posters. Browsing in the film section of a bookshop will quickly reveal several titles about the *Matrix* influence. You could buy *Taking the Red Pill* or *Is It Real?* to name but two. Luke (aged 16) wanted a full-length leather coat for Christmas 2001. A youth work conference in

---

[43] Interview in the *Independent on Sunday* Review, 2 August 2002.

early 2003 was called 'Matrix'. In the closing moments of *Big Brother 4* Davina McCall wore a T-shirt bearing witness to her pregnancy with the words 'Big Mother' on the front and 'reloaded' on the back. *The Matrix* has become a cultural phenomenon.

Yet *The Matrix* was a slow-burner. There was comparatively little pre-movie buzz about the first film. To some extent it was hiding behind the recently reinvigorated *Star Wars* franchise. *The Matrix* had a relatively poor opening weekend, grossing $28m (*The Matrix Reloaded* did $92m and broke records). But the reviews were good. The team from film magazine *Empire* were blown away; witness the end of their original review:

> *The Matrix* is about pure experience; it's been many a moon since the Empire crew have spilled out of a cinema literally buzzing with the sensation of a movie, babbling frenetically with the sheer excitement of discovery.
>
> From head to tail, the deliciously inventive Wachowskis (watch them skyrocket) have delivered the syntax for a new kind of movie: technically mind-blowing, style merged perfectly with content and just so damn cool, the usher will have to drag you kicking and screaming back into reality. You can bet your bottom dollar George never saw this phantom menace coming.[44]

By October 2001 *Empire* readers were voting *The Matrix* the fifth best movie of all time, behind *The Godfather* (1972), *The Shawshank Redemption* (1994), *The Empire Strikes Back* (1980) and *Star Wars* (1977).

[44] www.empireonline.co.uk/reviews

Critical mass

The Matrix managed to scrape itself over a 'tipping point' (that is, a point beyond which nothing could stop it being successful). Once there it started to provide a cultural backdrop and people wanted to emulate its style, colour, fashion, sound bites, moves and themes. The happenstance of this can be a matter of pure luck. Sure, the Wachowskis believed in their product, but the merchandise tie-ins were a bit late on the scene.

Ever since the invention of the teenager in the 1950s (the word 'teenager' was first used in 1941) marketers of youth-friendly products have been searching for the next cool thing. As soon as they find it they take it away, package it and sell it back later at a profit. In this context it is hard to determine who made the *Matrix* movies into the huge influence they have become on popular culture. Someone started polishing it and selling it back. Eventually it tipped.

Why have the films made such a profound impact on so many people? One of the reasons has to be the sheer volume of signs, symbols and ideas that the *Matrix* makers have incorporated into their product. It is only necessary to notice one or two of these in order to believe that the film is talking your language. We all like to have our good taste affirmed. It is certain that *Matrix* movies have enough of these 'hooks' to catch a huge range of the public. And we're not simply talking about product placement (where manufacturers pay to have their products included in, and thus endorsed by, a movie). The Internet magazine *eonline*[45] listed the following:

[45] www.eonline.com/Features/Features/Heavewave2003/Movies/Matrix/index.html

- Alice in Wonderland gave us the white rabbit
- Plato gave us the allegory of the cave, taken up by St Paul in the New Testament, 'Now all we can see of God is like a cloudy picture in a mirror. Later we will see him face to face ...'[46]
- Greek mythology gave us the names Morpheus, Niobe and Persephone
- Sci-fi writer William Gibson coined the expression 'cyberspace'
- Christianity gave us the idea of a saviour who dies and is resurrected, plus the name of Trinity
- Judaism gave us a homeland called Zion and a king called Nebuchadnezzar
- The world of science increasingly offers us the idea of organic machines and the potential they have for getting out of control unless regulated
- French philosopher and sceptic Jean Baudrillard gave us the idea that all is simulation

Furthermore:

- The Kung-fu movies of the 1970s gave us the blue-print for most of the action scenes, particularly incorporating wire technology instead of the more usually preferred CGI
- Marvel Comics gave us the idea of a caped super-hero
- Cecil B. DeMille's various epics, especially his depiction of Sodom and Gomorrah, gave us the rock-concert-like mass orgy in Zion from *Reloaded*
- Fritz Lang's *Metropolis* (1927) gave us the urban skylines

So the *Matrix* deals in philosophy, religion, science,

[46] 1 Corinthians 13:12 (*Contemporary English Version*).

science fiction, mythology, comic books, film history and a tradition of fun-violence. Enough catchiness everybody?

A postmodern Trojan horse

Movie enthusiast and Christian Youth Worker Tim Sudworth[47] feels that the impact of the *Matrix* movies has been to package an obscure French philosophy without the audience realising.

He goes on to say, '[*The Matrix*] deals with [the issues] and packages them into a "pop" culture. Therefore you have young people and adults thinking about issues raised by the film which are really quite heavy. Packaged any other way they wouldn't have engaged with them at all. (Try reading any book by Zygmunt Bauman ...[48]) The ideas and ethos of the film are not new just sold better ... People are being made to think about post-modernism.'

So is this true? Was a whole generation of young adults yearning and longing to discuss issues of truth and reality and *The Matrix* simply provided a spring-board? Or were they just impressed with the 'look'. It's a hard call. Which of us can honestly say we act out of complete purity of motive? We may enjoy our philo-sophical musings over a post-movie drink but most of the early discussion will probably be about bullet-time and flo-mo – the Wachowskis' brilliant inventions to sharpen up their fight scenes.

The *Matrix* films do utilise some of the most complicated special visual effects ever.

[47] Tim is the Diocesan Youth Advisor for Guildford Diocese of the Church of England. His quotes are taken from an interview with me in August 2003.

[48] Zygmunt Bauman is Emeritus Professor of Sociology at the Universities of Leeds and Warsaw and has written some of the more influential modern books on sociology.

Discussion board democracy

The Wachowski brothers have also taken the step of avoiding commenting on their movies. This has certainly helped to fuel discussion. If the directors steer clear of talking about the meaning of the film then it allows speculation to avalanche. It undoubtedly allows all views to compete on an even footing. It is a much-discussed thesis in the art world that once placed in the public domain the artist loses any rights to control over the meaning of the piece. By not speaking about it the Wachowskis have surrendered influence as well as control. This allows a more open and interesting discussion to take place, as it does not appear we are all sitting and waiting for the teacher to give 'the right answer' once we have dried up.

Carrie-Anne Moss (who plays Trinity) commented on this in interview when asked about the biblical significance of her character's name. She said, 'I don't have an answer to it. But the [Wachowski] brothers didn't name her that for nothing, and I think all the speculation is great. That's exactly what it's meant to be. It's meant for people to think and wonder and project their ideas of things onto this. That's one of the reasons the brothers don't talk about the movies. They don't want to endow it with their point of view.'[49]

'The Wachowskis made it cool to be confounded.'[50] So silence from the ones who knew increased the hype. As did the now-famous gap. The Wachowskis originally pitched the *Matrix* trilogy to Warner Brothers who

---

[49] www.eonline.com/Features/Features/Heatwave2003/Movies/ Matrix/index. html. Interview by H. W. Fowler, 7 May 2003.

[50] Peter Rainer, *New York* magazine 26 May 2003 quoted at www.newyork-metro.com/nymetro/movies/reviews/n_8702

frustratingly refused to commit to three movies until they saw how well the first one performed. When *The Matrix* became the biggest success in their history they were naturally in a hurry to bring out a sequel. This time the Wachowskis had the negotiating power. They still had their story and they wanted to tell it. They were holding all the aces. Whilst the ever-growing army of fans of the first movie rewatched and discussed their newly purchased videos and DVDs, the wait was filled with speculation. It only helped the cause that much of the dialogue in that first film was cryptic. Phrases reeked of theology and philosophy yet weren't easily placeable. A new-born addict had to do research. Or talk. *Matrix* on-line chat rooms started to grow.

And this is what it is like to be postmodern. 'The fast-paced inventions of modernity provoked an intellectual crisis, whereby the rational was questioned. Modernism gave way to postmodernism with even greater change, and there were no longer any fixed points. Human discourse and experience are open, suggestive, playful and relational.'[51] Maybe in a world where we talk a lot and are encouraged to value no one view above any other, the *Matrix* movies crashed the party. Here is a film with enough views that everyone can own some of them.

It took four years for the second movie to hit multi-plexes yet this with the knowledge that the final part had already been shot and would be released after just six more months. If you want hype then this is how to get it.

So what of those million and a half websites? Inevitably there are many merchandising parasites

[51] Kevin O'Donnell, *A History of Ideas* (Lion Publishing, 2003).

alongside the official sites. And the wacky. You want to know about conspiracy theories, secret codes and subliminal messages then www is the place for you. Happy surfing. Don't have nightmares.

But there are so many sites where intelligent discussion is going on. Try The Movie Review Query Engine (www.mrqe.com) as a starting point. Or just trawl through Google one hundred at a time. You will encounter some unexpected themes, from the black world experience to vegetarianism. Taste, but don't swallow it all. If there aren't enough different views and opinions on line for you, then there will be a place where you can add your own. Probably in crayon.

Poly-vinyl is the new black

What of fashion? It has always been easier to respond to a changing culture with cloth rather than concrete, so clothes will usually lead the way in finding a route through a trend. Neo is sleek and basic black – crew neck, leather long coat or a cassock-like over-garment which enables him to mimic Batman. He is also Keanu Reeves who is, at the time of writing, one of the cool guys of the season. In a world where reviewers are fond of describing action movie actors in terms of asses kicked per minute Neo is off the scale. Trinity's patent-leather jumpsuits are hand-me-downs from a million fetishistic top-shelf videos. Does this mean that both male and female characters wear clothes that largely appeal to men? Hmm. Rather think it does. Discuss.

The below-ground dwellers of Zion don't get to look individually cool. That's because their main scene is a party, everyone apparently striving for that acceptable anonymity which makes the whole more important than the sum of its parts. Any club in town, any given Saturday night. In Zion you mosh in a dancing frenzy.

And everyone from Zion stepping out into the light of the Matrix has to put on shades. It's the rule. Don't ask why but it adds a certain celebrity chic. Sells shades too.

In the virtual world of the Matrix there is colour. And the people look more real. OK more normal. 'Something is awry when a sci-fi movie about technological alienation features human protagonists who are less lively than their computerized counterparts.'[52] The Architect is clean-cut and suited like a Bond villain. The Keymaker wears regulation far-eastern Mao-uniform. The Banshee Twins have bleached clothes to match their albino appearance. And dreads. Persephone has been moulded into a dress of cream latex. Agent Smith is a Blues Brother. Or a Man in Black. Wherever you look there is someone or something to copy. Only the Oracle lives in a cheap apartment and dresses in a forgetably average way. You just don't notice prophets' clothes do you? That's why John the Baptist got such bad reviews for wearing camel.

Product replacement

Some of the product tie-ins are very well thought through and executed; indeed they add something to the whole *Matrix* experience. Not just the shades and posters. *Enter the Matrix* is a clever twist on the puzzle/beat-'em-up computer game format. Hacking (in this case finding secret shortcuts and cheats) is positively encouraged and will enable the player to make progress in the game not possible through normal play.

[52] Peter Rainer, *op cit*.

The storyline echoes plot threads from *The Matrix Reloaded* and the Wachowskis have contributed material that cannot be found in any other format.

The Animatrix (2003) has also gone a long way to rescuing the short animated film. For those of us old enough to remember when a trip to the movies included a supporting feature as well it is good to see an interest in short-film making being resurrected. It consists of short stories by different directors set in the Matrix world, all of them conceived, commissioned and approved by the Wachowski brothers. Again there is intertwining with the narrative of *The Matrix Reloaded*. Download the first four from the Internet for free.[53]

The soundtrack is pretty pumped, inspired by Rage Against the Machine and Marilyn Manson. There are few chilled-out mixes so probably not something to play during that dinner party but it will, of course, ring bells with club culture all over the world.

How influential is the violence in the films? The 'enemy' is an army of computer-generated images that simply happen to be programmed to look like people. So it doesn't hurt to kill them. We are given permission not to mourn the death of anybody who might not be real, so we feel no pain. A dangerous fallacy to invade our consciousness. In the real world even bad guys feel pain and have families. On the other hand the fatalities to those from Zion involve real blood and bereavement. It is unlikely that kung-fu moves will be invading our high streets. The Wachowskis have kept it at arm's length. It is too unbelievable to copy. Once we saw Neo flying, virtually or not, in *The Matrix Reloaded* we

[53] www.intothematrix.com

realised he had ceased to be what we know as human. Diana West, however, writing in ChronWatch.com (a media watchdog and conservative news site, with a focus on the *San Francisco Chronicle*) cautions about the effect of all this on those whose mental stability is suspect.[54]

Faith or fiction?

So why did the films make such a profound impact on so many members of faith communities? What has been the religious impact? Has it, as Dr Ted Baehr[55] says, 'been to propagandize people with some kind of anti-Christian, unbiblical, irrational atheist humanism ...'? Princeton University's Cornel West[56] has apparently had long 'philosophical' discussions about reality and society with Larry and Andy Wachowski, the creators behind the movies. He told the *Los Angeles Times* in its May 20, 2003 issue, that *The Matrix Reloaded* offers '... a devastating critique of all salvation stories.'

Sounds a bit extreme? Frederica Mathewes-Green[57] said, '*The Matrix* is surely the most overanalyzed movie since they invented Christian film critics.' The more discussion any piece of art generates the more extreme the views it attracts. And of course the views at the extremities are always the ones that interest the media and develop follow-up. It has always been desperately difficult to stand on a soapbox and yell, 'I am a moderate.' Fact is that religious people, and perhaps

[54] www.chronwatch.com/content/contentDisplay.asp?aid=2858&mode=print
[55] of Ankerberg Theological Research Institute, Chattanooga.
[56] Cornel West is Professor of Religion and African American Studies at Princeton University. He plays a member of the Zion Council in *Reloaded and Revolutions*.
[57] www.christianitytoday.com/ct/2003/119/11.0.html

Christians in particular, found so many analogies, metaphors and parallels from their faith story in *The Matrix* that they used them, unashamedly, to bounce off into telling their own stories. Perhaps we should have spent a little more time analysing exactly what the films were saying rather than claiming them as our own, for *The Matrix Reloaded* did indeed start to confound expectations, and although *The Matrix Revolutions* saw an abundance of Neo-as-messiah references resurfacing, it fell a long way short of advocating the Christian faith. Nevertheless, Evangelical Christians in particular seek opportunities to talk about their faith in the light of the culture of the day, and have done ever since St Paul visited Athens.[58] The *Matrix* films offer plenty of scope for asking the question 'is this what you think the world is like?'

Morpheus presents Neo with the truth about his world by shedding light on the dark secrets that have troubled him for so long: 'You've felt it your entire life, that there's something wrong with the world. You don't know what it is, but it's there, like a splinter in your mind, driving you mad.' The *Matrix* trilogy doesn't necessarily take its viewers much further than, 'I am the way and the truth is out there.' *Matrix* messiahs are necessary and *Matrix* messiahs need to be cool. So do real ones. Perhaps we should look at the packaging.

What has The *Matrix* started us doing that we didn't have to do? Talking about messiahs. Good.

[58] Acts 17:16-34.

CHAPTER 6

The architects' foundations

by Peter S. Williams

It's the question that drives us.

If *The Matrix* were a delicatessen of the mind, it would be an American one. Philosophical sandwiches burst at the seams with rich, tasty concepts for us to eagerly devour and try to digest. So much is loaded on our plate,[59] that it's easy to fail to do justice to the whole meal. In this chapter, we will pick at some of the basic philosophical concepts and schools of thought that underpin the *Matrix* movies, as an aid to your digestive process. Here comes the condiment tray.

The question of meta-narratives

According to professor of English Dino Felluga, 'Few films in the Hollywood canon make as clear a direct reference to postmodern theory as does *The Matrix*.'[60] Postmodernism has been defined as 'scepticism towards meta-narratives'. A meta-narrative is an over-arching 'story' that sets up an explanatory context for understanding 'life, the universe, and everything'. In

---

[59] And it's a big plate.
[60] Dino Felluga, 'The Matrix: Paradigm of Postmodernity or Intellectual Poseur? Part 1', in *Taking the Red Pill*, Glenn Yeffeth (ed.) (Summersdale, 2003), p.85.

other words, it's a worldview communicated through a story. All religions and philosophies provide a meta-narrative. In Christianity, this takes the form of the story of creation, fall and recreation. Even postmodernism, which denies meta-narratives, provides one. The meta-narrative of postmodernism is that we should be sceptical of meta-narratives!

Nietzsche notoriously claimed that 'God is dead',[61] and the consequence of his claim has been the growing assumption that defines postmodernism, the belief that 'Truth is dead'. For example, postmodernist John Caputo asserts: 'The truth is that there is no truth.'[62] The two claims are not unrelated. As philosopher Peter Kreeft writes: 'God is objective spirit, and when "God is dead", the objective world is reduced to matter and the spiritual world is reduced to subjectivity ... '[63]

Watching *The Matrix* induces a sort of 'truth-vertigo' in us, where we become suspicious of any and all claims to truth as the Wachowski brothers subvert our assumptions about the reality presented to us in the films. As successive layers of deception and unreality peel away like the layers of an onion, we are forced to ask whether there is any fundamental reality (in the films or in real life) that could be expressed in a meta-narrative, or whether life is, as it were, onion all the way down! As Morpheus asks at the end of the human-machine war in *The Matrix Revolutions*: 'Is this real?' Postmodernism amounts to accepting that reality is like

[61] Nietzsche actually put the famous phrase in the mouth of a character in his book *The Gay Science* (1882).

[62] Quoted by William Lane Craig in *Five Views on Apologetics*, Steven B. Cowan (ed.) (Zondervan, 2000), p.45.

[63] Peter Kreeft, *Heaven – The Heart's Deepest Longing* (Ignatius Press, 1989), p.23.

an infinite onion: however many layers of deceptive unreality we 'see through', we can never reach a knowable prime reality.

The question of truth

More fundamental than the question 'What is the truth?' is the question Pilate asked Jesus: 'What is truth?' (John 18:38). Aristotle pointed out that: 'If one says of what is that it is, or of what is not that it is not, he speaks the truth; but if one says of what is that it is not, or of what is not that it is, he does not speak the truth.'[64] This is the common-sense 'correspondence' definition of truth. If Neo is 'the One' and Morpheus believes that Neo is the One, then Morpheus' belief that Neo is 'the One' is true. One might think that the nature of truth was straightforward and obvious enough, but as philosopher Arthur F. Holmes laments, today:

> ... an adequate conception of truth itself is largely lost ... In a *uni*verse subject to the rule of one creator-God ... truth is seen as an interrelated and coherent whole ... But whenever the focus on truth is lost, our loss includes the unity of truth: and when the universality of truth is lost, it includes the universal truth of any one unifying world-view. What then happens to truth in relation to art and morals? ... We are left with fragmented items devoid of any ultimate coherence.[65]

The postmodern rejection of truth is the outworking of the modernist's rejection of God, a rejection that results

---

[64] Quoted by Peter Kreeft, *Between Heaven and Hell* (InterVarsity Press, 1982).

[65] Arthur F. Holmes, *All Truth is God's Truth* (InterVarsity Press, 1979), p.6-7.

in the loss of objective goodness and beauty as well as truth.

Nietzsche presented the world with the characteristically postmodern theory of 'perspectivism': 'There are many kinds of eyes, and consequently there are many kinds of "truths", and consequently there is no truth.'[66] Nietzsche doesn't simply claim that different people have different opinions (Morpheus believes that the prophecy of the One is true, Lock doesn't. At least one of them must be wrong); rather, he claims that the truth that different people have different opinions means that it is true that there is no truth! Thus Nietzsche drains the world of an objective God and objective truth in one foul swoop. This denial of truth is embodied by Cypher, who treacherously swaps the harsh reality of life aboard the *Nebuchadnezzar* for the comfortable illusion of life in the Matrix. After all, what is truth? Cypher becomes 'Like a hungry man dreaming he's eating steak' (Isaiah 29:8). Of course, if Nietzsche is claiming that his state- ment is *true*, then it is most certainly false, because it contradicts itself (if there is no truth, how can it be true that there is no truth?). On the other hand, if he is not claiming to know the truth that there is no absolute truth, then he most certainly cannot be contradicting anyone who claims that there is such a thing as absolute truth, whether about God or anything else. Either way, Nietzsche's 'perspectivism' falls by the wayside.

Aristotle didn't *invent* the meaning of 'truth', he *dis- covered* it. Saying that a proposition is 'true' is just say- ing that the world is as that proposition would have you believe it to be: 'truth is what corresponds to reality,

[66] Quoted by Os Guinness, *Time for Truth: Living Free in a World of Lies, Hype and Spin* (Baker Books, 2002), p.31.

what corresponds to the state of affairs about which that statement is being made.'[67] To say that this definition of truth 'is not true' is to inadvertently affirm that it *is* true by relying upon the very notion one is denying! As Peter Kreeft and Ronald Tacelli write:

> All theories of truth, once they are expressed clearly and simply, presuppose the commonsensical notion of truth that is enshrined in the wisdom of language and the tradition of usage, namely the correspondence ... theory. For each theory claims that it is really true, that is, that it corresponds to reality, and that the others are really false, that is, that they fail to correspond to reality.[68]

The question of knowledge

The Greek philosopher Plato told an allegorical story called 'The Cave' that went something like this:

> Imagine prisoners chained in such a way that they face the back wall of a cave. They have always been there, and see nothing of themselves or each other; they see only shadows on the wall of the cave cast by a fire that burns behind them. Between the fire and the prisoners are paraded various objects, and the prisoners naturally mistake the shadows of these objects on the wall of the cave for reality. Suppose one prisoner escaped his chains, turned around and looked at the true source of the shadows. The fire temporarily pains his eyes; and he prefers the pleasant deception of the dark. But the prisoner stumbles out of the

[67] Norman L. Geisler, *The Issue of Truth*, Tape, Side 1.
[68] Peter Kreeft and Ronald Tacelli, *Handbook of Christian Apologetics* (InterVarsity Press, 1994), p.366.

cave into the world beyond of trees and mountains, rivers and sky, into the blinding sunlight. As his eyes adjust he finally sees the sun, the source of all light.

Plato suggested that if this enlightened man were to return to the prisoners in the cave and tell them about the real world he would appear ridiculous. They might even kill him for attempting to disturb their illusions. Plato used this allegory to highlight the distinction between appearance and reality (things are not always as they appear to be). Light represents truth and the shadows represent delusion. The prisoner who escapes from the cave represents Plato's teacher Socrates, who was executed by the state for asking too many questions! The parallels between Plato's Cave and the Wachowski's Matrix are obvious, as Thomas Anderson is dragged out of the illusion of the 'cave' and into the harsh, bright light of reality. Much later, when Neo and Trinity reach the Machine City in *Matrix Revolutions*, Neo exclaims 'It's unbelievable Trin, light everywhere, like the whole thing was built of light.' This, it would seem, is reality.

Descartes' demon of doubt

*Have you ever had a dream, Neo, that you were
so sure was real? What if you were unable to
wake from that dream, Neo? How would you
know the difference between the dream world
and the real world?*
MORPHEUS, *THE MATRIX*

French philosopher Rene Descartes (1596-1650), in search of knowledge that was beyond all possibility of doubt, employed the thought experiment of imagining that there existed a powerful evil demon, hell-bent on deceiving him about as much as possible. Descartes concluded that a demon could not possibly deceive him about his own existence, or the existence of God (whose existence Descartes sought to prove from the fact of his own consciousness and the indubitable contents thereof). Descartes argued that, since he could be absolutely certain, on pain of self-contradiction, that he was thinking ('I think, therefore I am'), and since he could not be absolutely certain on pain of self-contradiction that he had a body (an evil demon could be deceiving him about this, but not about the fact that he was thinking), he could be certain that his thoughts were not identical with his body. Having got to this point, Descartes was left with the problem of how our knowledge of the physical world could be validated. Descartes thought that the existence of God rescues us from scepticism about the natural world, because God, being good, would not allow us to be systematically deceived about what our senses tell us.[69]

The same questions about the reliability of human knowledge are asked by philosophers today, only now those questions are asked in the context of evolutionary theory. Some philosophers argue that it doesn't seem likely that natural selection alone can account for human cognitive capacities. As Richard Rorty writes: 'The idea that one species of organism is, unlike all the others, oriented not just towards its own increased prosperity but towards Truth, is as un-Darwinian as the idea that every human being has a built-in moral compass

[69] cf. Rene Descartes, *Meditations* at http://philos.wright.edu/DesCartes/Meditations.html

– a conscience that swings free of both social history and individual luck.'[70] But as Alvin Plantinga replies,[71] this is a self-defeating claim, in that it gives one reason to doubt the naturalistic worldview upon which it is based (and hence some reason to accept a theistic worldview). As Douglas Groothuis argues: 'If the universe was not made for us in mind, if there is no created "fit" between our mind and our world, then there is no reason to trust our mind's apprehension of the universe.'[72] If the universe *was* made with us in mind, then it is a universe of knowable objective truth centred in the being of God.

A major stream of contemporary epistemology (theory of knowledge) is 'reformed epistemology'. The basic idea of reformed epistemology is that our beliefs are generally reliable because our minds have, as Descartes thought, been purposefully designed to give us knowledge. However, reformed epistemologists point out that Descartes' insistence on basing *all* knowledge on undoubtable foundations is too restrictive. Why should the burden of proof be on us to prove such common-sense beliefs as the existence of a physical world, rather than on the sceptic who suggests that there is not? As well as such indubitable beliefs as 'I think, therefore I am', we have many 'properly basic' beliefs that we are perfectly within our rights to believe even though it isn't self-contradictory to doubt them. For example, we lack conclusive proof that our bodies are not merely computer generated illusions (any evidence offered for this belief could be part of the illusion), but that doesn't

---

[70] Richard Rorty, 'Untruth and Consequences', *The New Republic*, 31 July 1995, p.36.

[71] Alvin Plantinga, *Warrant and Proper Function* (Oxford, 1993).

[72] Douglas Groothuis, *Truth Decay* (InterVarsity Press, 2000), p.45. cf. Peter S. Williams, *The Case for God* (Monarch, 1999), p.236-249.

make it irrational to assume that our bodies are precisely what they appear to be.

The question of consciousness

The possibility of machines attaining consciousness is more than just a staple of science fiction. Many thinkers and researchers believe that what is present day science fiction may become reality in the not too distant future. Artificial intelligence guru Ray Kurzweil:

> ... believes that with neurological architecture, sufficient complexity, and the right combination of analog and digital processes, computers will become 'spiritual' like we are. His references to spirituality might lead one to suspect that he departs from naturalism. But Kurzweil is careful with his definition. By saying computers will become spiritual, he means that they will become *conscious*. While this differs from the arid materialism of Daniel Dennet, Steven Pinker and Richard Dawkins, who treat consciousness as an illusion, the identification of the spirit with consciousness is a naturalistic stratagem.[73]

The difference between 'consciousness' and 'spirit' (or 'soul') is significant. As J. P. Moreland explains:

> Historically and biblically, Christianity has held to a dualistic notion of the human being. A human being is a unity of two distinct realities – body and soul. More specifically, I *am* my soul and I *have* my body. The soul, while not by nature immortal, is nevertheless capable of entering into an intermediate disembodied state upon death and, eventually, being reunited with a resurrected body.[74]

[73] William A. Dembski.

The belief that humans just are their physical bodies is called physicalism. Physicalism is a natural result of a naturalistic worldview, because naturalism rejects the existence of anything besides the natural world. Physicalism is part and parcel of the naturalist's rejection of God (after all, if one has reason to think that God exists, then one has less reason to deny that the human mind could be non-physical) and physicalism is a testing-ground for naturalism. If naturalism fails to account for the mind, then naturalism fails (something explored in chapter 9).[75]

Rather than *explaining* consciousness, naturalists end up *denying* it by telling us that consciousness, far from requiring the existence of a spiritual substance (an immaterial 'mind' or 'soul') is 'nothing but physical events in my brain and nervous system'.[76]

Francis Crick advances the *Astonishing Hypothesis* that: 'your joys and your sorrows, your memories and your ambitions, your sense of personal identity and free will, are in fact no more than the behaviour of a vast assembly of nerve cells and their assorted molecules. As Lewis Carroll's Alice might have phrased it: "You're nothing but a pack of neurons." '[77] Crick advances his hypothesis in the name of science and in opposition to the religious view 'that some kind of spirit exists that

---

[74] J. P. Moreland, *Love Your God With All Your Mind: The Role of Reason in the Life of the Soul* (NavPress, 1997), p.68.

[75] 'Dualism supports belief in a transcendent realm of reality. Dualism breaks the stranglehold of scientism and physicalism and supports belief in God and a transcendent dimension of reality ... The existence of at least one non-physical, non-empirical reality opens up the door for the claim that there is an entire transcendent domain of reality.' – Gary R. Habermas and J. P. Moreland, *Beyond Death* (Crossway, 1998), p.108.

[76] Jaegwon Kim, *Mind in a Physical World: An Essay on the Body-Mind Problem and Mental Causation* (MIT Press, 1998), p.43.

[77] Francis Crick, *The Astonishing Hypothesis – The Scientific Search for the Soul* (Simon & Schuster, 1994), p.3.

persists after one's bodily death and, to some degree, embodies the essence of that human being.'[78] But how can science disprove the existence of the human spirit (which, being immaterial is scientifically un-detectable in itself)? Is Crick's physicalism even a coherent possibility? After all, how much store should we set by a hypothesis advanced by nothing but a pack of neurons?

Materialists work on the unproven assumption that the reality of consciousness can be squared with naturalism, ruling out mind-body dualism from the start and then seeking to explain mere consciousness within materialistic categories. But as naturalist Ned Block admits:

> We have no conception of our physical or functional nature that allows us to understand how it could explain our subjective experience ... we have nothing – zilch – worthy of being called a research programme, nor are there any substantive proposals about how to go about starting one ... Researchers are *stumped*.[79]

It is hardly surprising to find philosopher of mind John Heil reporting that: 'In recent years, dissatisfaction with materialist assumptions has led to a revival of interest in forms of dualism.'[80]

The question of choice

The 'nothing buttery' that characterises naturalistic accounts of consciousness has implications for questions about free will (if true, then we have no free will) and morality (if we have no free choice we have no

[78] Francis Crick, *The Astonishing Hypothesis*, p.3-4.

[79] Ned Block, 'Consciousness' in *A Companion to the Philosophy of Mind*, Samuel Guttenplan (ed.) (Blackwell, 1994), p.211.

[80] John Heil, *Philosophy of Mind: A Contemporary Introduction* (Routledge, 1998), p.53.

moral responsibility). Questions about the reality and significance of choice (and so the truth of naturalism and physicalism) run through the *Matrix* trilogy. *The Matrix Revolutions* suggests that we do have free choice ('Because I choose to' replies Neo to Agent Smith's taunts), but leaves open the question of whether the only significant thing about choice is the mere fact *that we choose* (the philosophy of 'existentialism'), or whether it actually matters what we choose because, despite Smith's taunts ('Do you believe you're fighting for something? For more than your survival? Can you tell me what it is? Do you even know? Is it freedom? Or truth? Perhaps peace? Yes? No? Could it be for love? Illusions, Mr Anderson, vagaries of perception.'), some things do matter objectively.

To reverse the question, if some things really do matter, such that we genuinely *ought* to choose them, doesn't this show that there must be more to consciousness than a pack of neurons? There are two significant facts about moral laws. First of all, moral laws, unlike physical laws, are laws or commands that we *ought* to obey (it makes no sense to say that a machine morally *ought* to perform its function, because it *has* to perform its function according to the laws of nature). Secondly, moral laws, unlike physical laws, are commands *that we have a choice about obeying* (a machine has no choice about obeying the law of gravity, but we must have a choice about obeying the moral law against murder if we are to be truly responsible for obeying it or not). If we have no choice about obeying moral laws, then it makes no sense to say that we *ought* to obey them. Therefore, if we *ought* to obey a moral law, then we must have a choice about obeying it. Physicalism reduces and restricts consciousness to naturalistic categories, and since nature knows nothing of responsibility or choice, the reality of the moral *ought* implies the reality of free choice (like Neo's choice to sacrifice himself to end the machine-human war, giving one and all a free choice of destiny), thereby disproving Crick's astonishing hypothesis.[81] The question is whether or not there is a real moral law, whether there are any choices that we morally ought to make or not to make.

Moral oughts, if they exist, would define our purpose in the sense of defining what we ought to do. Agent Smith begins the *Matrix* trilogy with a function (to be an agent of the system), but, as a machine constructed by rogue machines, it is arguable that he has no purpose, in the sense that there is nothing that he ought to choose. In the end, Smith denies the existence of any purpose for life, saying that the only 'purpose' of life 'is to end'. There is nothing one ought to aim for, and even love is dismissed as a spurious meaning. It is a meaning Trinity embraces wholeheartedly: 'I wished I had the chance to say what really mattered. To say I loved you.' It is a meaning that motivates Neo (e.g. when he chooses to rescue Morpheus in *The Matrix* and Trinity in *The Matrix Reloaded*), who as the 'mirror image' of Smith begins the *Matrix* trilogy unaware of his purpose, but finds purpose in choosing to obey his calling to be 'the

[81] It also implies that the moral law must be commanded by a personal reality worthy of obedience. You can't have moral laws without a moral lawgiver. And since the moral law transcends human individuals, and even the state, so too must the moral lawgiver. cf. William Lane Craig, 'The Indispensability of Theological Meta-Ethical Foundations for Morality' at www.leaderu.com/offices/billcraig/docs/meta-eth.html; C. S. Lewis, 'Right and Wrong as Clues to the Heart of the Universe' at www.mit.edu/~mcguyton/ABSK/MereChristianity/meretoc.htm; J. P. Moreland, 'The Ethical Inadequacy of Naturalism' at www.afterall.net/citizens/moreland/papers/jp-naturalism2.html

One'. This choice is driven by Neo's love for humanity in general, and Morpheus and Trinity in particular, despite all the hardships his vocation entails.

Welcome to the desert of the real

When Morpheus reveals the real world to Neo in *The Matrix* he says, 'Welcome to the desert of the real'. *The Matrix* presents knowing the truth about reality as an important human goal and need, but one that takes courage to pursue. Self-delusion is comforting, especially when reality is harsh; but following the 'will to truth' like the inhabitants of Zion is morally heroic, whilst following the 'will to personal gratification' (like the hedonistic Cypher) or 'the will to power' (like the nihilistic Smith) at the expense of truth is seen to be morally perverse. Truth is ultimately more powerful than the matrix of lies we culpably accept (whether from others or from ourselves), because truth allows us to operate within, and so to co-operate with, reality. Those who take the 'blue pill', those who set their heart on dessert (pleasure, power, etc) rather than on truth (as Neo does when he takes the 'red pill') get their just deserts. By failing to engage truthfully with reality they actually fail to engage with the true reality of the dessert they have set their heart upon. In lying to themselves, they end up living a lie. To live out a perversion of truth in this way is inevitably to pervert one's very self. Cypher becomes superficial; Smith becomes seriously unhinged. Setting the heart upon truth, on the other hand, may involve facing up to uncomfortable truths (even about ourselves), but offers the only possibility of living with the reality beyond the matrix of lies, spin and self-deception.

CHAPTER 7

This is the construct: Postmodernism and *The Matrix*

by Tony Watkins

I imagine that right now you are feeling a bit like Alice, tumbling down the rabbit hole?

After the first film of the trilogy, it seemed like different groups of people claimed *The Matrix* for their own. Many Christians jumped up and down with glee at the Christian names, metaphors and concepts within the film, some even arguing that it was a Christian film. But at the same time there were Buddhists, Hindus and Gnostics who found it to be rich with concepts from their own worldview. Fans of Greek myths and Arthurian legends have also been pleased. Slavojzizek wrote that it 'functions as a kind of Rorschach [ink blot] test, setting in motion the universalized process of recognition ... practically every orientation seems to recognize itself in it.'[82]

But underpinning all these disparate elements which the Wachowskis have built into their films,[83] are

---

[82] Slavojzizek, 'The Matrix: Or, the Two Sides of Perversion' in *The Matrix and Philosophy: Welcome to the Desert of the Real*, William Irwin (ed.) (Chicago: Open Court, 2002) p.240-241.

[83] The Wachowski brothers have insisted that all elements of philosophy, mythology, theology, etc. are there deliberately. A cynic might wonder whether it's easy for them to say this in response to anybody finding one of their pet subjects included. I'm not a cynic; I think they're telling the truth.

postmodern foundations. This reveals itself in a number of interrelated ways. First, there's the overriding importance of the media for people within the Matrix. Literally every sensation of their entire lives comes to them through the total media, which is the Matrix 'neural-interactive simulation'. One way of reading *The Matrix*, which was quite common after the first film, was as a critique of media-saturated western – specifically American – culture. The final resolution of *The Matrix Revolutions* could be seen as undermining this reading – at least to some extent. Rather than a call to resist the media system, it becomes an invitation to reach some kind of synergy.

Second, is the Matrix as a system of control or of 'ideology', by which postmodernists tend to mean the system of rules, language, signs and beliefs that structure and shape our lives. The Matrix shapes the lives of its inhabitants – it creates their 'reality'. It is a way of keeping the occupants of pods functioning so that the machines could exploit their resources.[84] *The Matrix* can then be seen as an attack on the way that the global capitalist machine, through the media and entertainment industry, fulfils our desires in order to exploit our resources. *The Matrix Reloaded* intensifies this. First, with Neo's discovery that the Oracle is part of the system of control. Second, with the Architect's revelation that the One is a 'systemic anomaly' in the Matrix, whose function is to 'return to the Source, allowing a temporary dissemination of the code [he carries],

---

[84] Contrary to what Morpheus believes, the humans are not for generating electricity for the machines – they would need to be given more energy than they would return to the system. It's more likely that their brains are hooked up to become a vast parallel processing computer.

reinserting the prime program.' In other words, Neo himself is caught up in the system of control. This rabbit hole goes deeper than Morpheus had even dreamt of.

Third, the end of the story shows a move from hostility between controllers and controlled, to a recognition of interdependence. In doing so it introduces another key postmodern element: the equal validity of radically different perspectives. It's OK to be a machine or a human, within the mainstream system of the Matrix or out of it. What matters is peace and harmony. This is the reason for the wide range of religious imagery and ideas within the trilogy – the Wachowskis seem to want a synthesis between eastern religion (represented by Hinduism and Buddhism) and 'western' religion (represented by Christianity and Gnosticism).

Fourth, *The Matrix* is an exploration of the postmodern tension between what is real and what is a representation. This is the area on which this chapter will focus.

Baudrillard basics

The Matrix is responsible for introducing a vast audience to the ideas of French thinker Jean Baudrillard (pronounced bode-ree-yar).[85] They permeate the film and, perhaps, are one of the biggest influences on the Wachowskis' writing. Before he was even allowed to read the script, Andy and Larry Wachowski made Keanu Reeves read Baudrillard's *Simulacra and Simulation* (1983).

---

[85] There are other discernible academic influences – the Frankfurt School and Jacques Lacan, for example. For information on Lacan's influence on the *Matrix* films, see Dino Felluga, 'The Matrix: Paradigm of postmodernism or intellectual poseur? Part I' in *Taking the Red Pill*, Glenn Yeffeth (ed.) (Summersdale, 2003), pp.85-101; Slavojzizek, 'The Matrix: Or, the Two Sides of Perversion' in *The Matrix and Philosophy*, William Irwin (ed.) (Chicago: Open Court, 2002), pp.240-241.

Jean Baudrillard (1929-) is a French sociologist and one of the most significant of all postmodern theorists. He is famous for insisting in the French newspaper *Liberation* that the 1991 Gulf War did not happen.[86] You'll immediately appreciate that he has a fondness for making his points in extreme and provocative ways. This is more than simply a desire to be annoying; he believes that it is only by taking up extreme positions that it is possible to stop culture imploding. He also seems to like making his points in almost impenetrable ways, often not bothering to explain the obscure words he uses or even those he invents. My guess is, nobody truly understands what Baudrillard is saying. Except Baudrillard. And I'm not too sure about him. There are times reading Baudrillard's writing when I find myself at least wondering if he's really saying anything of significance at all or just stringing together a lot of impressive sounding words.

But Baudrillard has become very influential in popular culture. In the days when access to academic ideas was very limited, ideas were slow to trickle down from the universities into the general culture. But now the people who most directly influence society are those in the media. Many creative people like the Wachowskis will have been taught Baudrillard, Foucault, Derrida and others at college not very long ago. They have absorbed and assimilated postmodern theory, and are now communicating it in their television series, books and films. Ideas like

[86] His point is that we are totally dependent on the media for our knowledge of it and we can't verify what the media tells us. See also his book, *The Gulf War did not Take Place* (Indiana University Press, 1995).

those of Baudrillard underpin films like *The Truman Show*, *Minority Report*, *Pleasantville*, and others.[87]

Simulacra and Simulation

Baudrillard's best-known book is *Simulacra and Simulation* – a collection of essays published in 1983 about the nature of what we perceive to be reality. He starts with a story told by Jorge Luis Borges[88]: The cartographers of a certain empire wanted to make the most accurate map of the empire they possibly could. They constructed larger and larger maps with more and more detail. The day came when they made a map so detailed that it exactly covered the empire and obscured the territory underneath. Borges writes, 'Less addicted to the study of Cartography, the Following Generations comprehended that this dilated Map was Useless and, not without Impiety, delivered it to the Inclemencies of the Sun and of the Winters,' until at last only a few shreds are left in the deserts. Baudrillard turns this round to say, 'today, it is the territory whose shreds slowly rot across the extent of the map. It is the real, and not the map, whose vestiges persist in the deserts that are no longer those of the Empire, but ours. *The desert of the real itself* ... In fact, even inverted, Borges' fable is unusable ... it is no longer a question of either maps or territories. Something has disappeared: the sovereign difference, between one and the other, that constituted the charm of abstraction ... It is no longer a question of imitation, nor duplication, nor even parody. It is a question of substituting the signs of the real for the real.'[89]

---

[87] For a number of other examples, see Tony Watkins, 'Blurring Boundaries' at www.damaris.org/content/content.php?type=5&id=205

[88] The story appears in Jorge Luis Borges' and Adolfo Casares' *Extraordinary Tales* (Allison & Busby, 1990).

Baudrillard is saying that this is the kind of situation in which we live; this is what our world is like. We have a world that is so overwhelmed by signs, by representations of reality – through television, the Internet, etc. – that we've reached the point where we can no longer tell the difference between what's real and what's a simulation. We've lost touch with reality and rely on models and maps instead. The simulation is so seductive, exciting and glossy that we don't really care about reality. In fact, he goes on to say, we've reached the point where there is no reality left. All we have is what Baudrillard calls the hyperreal – everything is just simulations (maps if you like), but simulations which don't refer to some more fundamental reality – what he calls *simulacra*.

The hyperreal has become all-important

Baudrillard talks about the 'three orders of simulacra':

First order — The image is clearly a copy of the real. It represents the real but people are in no doubt about what it is. Baudrillard associated this with the pre-modern period.

Second order — Technology makes possible a perfect imitation. Mass production means there are lots of near-identical copies of things. The underlying reality can

---

[89] Jean Baudrillard, *Simulacra and Simulation*, Sheila Glaser (tr.) (University of Michigan Press, 1994), p.2. Interestingly, Baudrillard apparently didn't spot that the story of the mapmakers illustrates his ideas about simulations of a non-existent reality at another level. Borges and Casares attributed the story to a seventeenth-century writer named Suarez Miranda who doesn't seem to have existed. The story, then, is a simulacrum – a simulation of something that doesn't exist.

	be misrepresented or masked because it is imitated so well. This is associated with the industrial revolution of the nineteenth century.
Third order	Now in the postmodern age, we have to contend with what he calls the 'precession of simulacra'. In other words, the representation comes first and is more important. The distinction between reality and its representation has gone and an image 'has no relation to any reality whatsoever: it is its own pure simulacrum.'[90]

But how does any of this – or Baudrillard's other influential ideas – come into *The Matrix* trilogy?

Baudrillard's ideas in *The Matrix*
Simulacra and Simulation
The first direct reference to Baudrillard comes early on in the film when some people arrive at computer hacker Neo's room to pick up some computer code he has worked on. Neo takes a book from a shelf and removes a storage device containing the code from the space hollowed out within the book. We see briefly that the book is *Simulacra and Simulation*,[91] open to the chapter 'On Nihilism'. There's a very deliberate irony here: what Neo picks up is not a real book, but a simulation of one. Within it is stored code, which is a central idea in much of Baudrillard's work (see below).

---

[90] Jean Baudrillard, *Simulacra and Simulation*, p.6.

[91] Another book has a brief cameo: in *The Matrix Reloaded*, Persephone uses Arthur Schopenhauer's *Die Welt Als Wille Und Vorstellung* (The World as Will and Conception) to open the secret door.

The desert of the real

Another clear reference to Baudrillard comes when Morpheus talks to Neo within the Construct. Neo is shocked to find himself standing in a pure white space which is empty of everything except two red leather armchairs and a television. Morpheus sits in one of the chairs and turns on the television[92] to show scenes of Chicago in 1999. This is the world Neo *thought* he lived in. But then the scene changes to one of complete desolation. We zoom into the scene and down from the sky to find that Morpheus and Neo are now in the scene. As Neo staggers at this transformation, Morpheus says to him, 'Welcome to the desert of the real.' This is a direct quotation from page 1 of an essay in *Simulacra and Simulation* called 'The Precession of Simulacra'.

'On Nihilism'

It is no accident that the chapter at which Neo opens his hollow copy of *Simulacra and Simulation* is 'On Nihilism'. This is actually the last chapter of the book, but Neo opens his fake volume near the beginning to access the cavity inside. And the first page of a chapter usually appears on the right hand side of a book, not the left as it does in this scene. This is flagging up the significance of the chapter for those who notice. In it, Baudrillard says, 'Everywhere, always, the system is too strong: hegemonic.' He declares himself to be a nihilist and says that the only response to the controlling system is terrorism. He claims to be 'a terrorist and nihilist in [the realm of] theory as the

---

[92] Notice that it's an old television but with a remote control. This is deliberate because the model is significant – it's a Radiola 'Deep View'.

others are with their weapons. Theoretical violence, not truth, is the only resource left to us.'[93]

Within the *Matrix* trilogy, terrorism is, of course, the only strategy which seems open to Morpheus and his crew. When we first see Thomas Anderson asleep in front of his PC, the screen is showing news reports of a manhunt for Morpheus after an incident at Heathrow airport. So Baudrillard apparently gives an intellectual justification for the Wachowskis to make a film that revolves around violence (not that they need one – as chapter 1 shows, they came to the *Matrix* trilogy from a world of anime and comic books). But bear in mind that Baudrillard may be teasing us again when he asserts that terrorism is the only response – he really wants to make a point about using academic theory to attack the system of late capitalism.

The virtual world

However, the link with Baudrillard goes way beyond these references, which could simply be respectful nods in his direction. In *The Matrix* shooting script, the connection was made very explicit. After saying, 'Welcome to the desert of the real,' Morpheus was to have added, 'You have been living in a dreamworld, Neo. As in Baudrillard's vision, your whole life has been spent inside the map not the territory. This is the world as it exists today. The "desert of the real".'[94]

I haven't come across any explanation about why this line was dropped. Maybe the reference to Baudrillard himself would have sounded out of place or pretentious.

[93] Jean Baudrillard, *Simulacra and Simulation*, p.163.
[94] Andy and Larry Wachowski, *The Matrix: The Shooting Script* (Newmarket Press, 2001), p.38.

But it may be that the references to map and territory (referring, of course, to the Borges fable which Baudrillard retells) give the wrong idea. The map remains a representation of the real, although (in Baudrillard's inversion of the tale) the real has become a desert. This could possibly make the Matrix function as a second order simulation in Baudrillard's framework (above) rather than as a third order simulacrum. Indeed, Baudrillard himself seems to have viewed *The Matrix* in this way and is therefore critical of it.

Baudrillard's perspective on *The Matrix*

Referring to the brief cameo of *Simulacra and Simulation*, Brent Staples wrote in the *New York Times* that:

> Most writers would swoon over product placement like this. But Mr. Baudrillard was unimpressed when we conversed by e-mail recently. He noted that the film's 'borrowings' from his work 'stemmed mostly from misunderstandings' and suggested that no movie could ever do justice to the themes of this book. This sounds like a parody of a French intellectual, but it also happens to be true.[95]

James McGrath comments that 'the only Baudrillard most people will ever know is what they have understood from and/or in light of *The Matrix*. Somehow it seems fundamentally appropriate, albeit also rather disturbing, that the philosopher who warned us of the dangers of technological simulacra should find himself and his thoughts obscured in precisely the fashion he predicted.

---

[95] 'A French Philospher Talks Back to Hollywood and The Matrix', *New York Times*, 24 May 2002.

"Fate, it seems, is not without a sense of irony." '[96]

In an interview given after *The Matrix Reloaded* was released, Baudrillard explains how he thinks Andy and Larry Wachowski misunderstood him:

> The Wachowski staff did contact me after the first episode to involve me in the following ones, but that really was not conceivable! What we have here is essentially the same misunderstanding as with the simulationist artists in New York in the '80s. These people take the hypothesis of the virtual as a fact and carry it over to visible phantasms. But the primary characteristic of this universe lies precisely in the inability to use categories of the real to speak about it ... Anyway, the real nuisance in this movie is that the brand-new problem of the simulation is mistaken with the very classic problem of the illusion, already mentioned by Plato. Here lies the mistake.[97]

What Baudrillard seems to be saying is that the Wachowskis were still talking in the wrong categories – a virtual reality illusion (the Matrix) *in contrast* to a real reality to which rebels could escape. Baudrillard claims we cannot access reality, and therefore everything is illusion, everything is simulation. Illusion becomes a meaningless idea when there is no real against which to compare it. Virtual reality implies the

---

[96] James McGrath, 'The Desert of the Real: Christianity, Buddhism & Baudrillard in *The Matrix* films and popular culture' from the conference *Visions of Humanity in Cyberculture, Cyberspace and Science Fiction* (Monday 11 August – Wednesday 13 August 2003, Prague) – www.inter-disciplinary. net/ati/Visions/V1/mcgrath%20paper.pdf

[97] *Le Nouvel Observateur*, no. 2015, 19 June 2003. There is an English translation of this interview at www.teaser.fr/~lcolombet/empyree/divers/Matrix-Baudrillard_english.html, and you'll find the original at www.nouvelobs.com/dossiers/p2015/a201937.html

existence of reality. But Baudrillard's point is that *there is no reality*, only hyperreality. *The Matrix* asks questions about what is real, but for Baudrillard they are non-questions.[98]

The Matrix as third order simulacrum

But I wonder whether Baudrillard misread the first film. The Matrix may, in fact, be considered as a third order simulation (see above) – a simulacrum, i.e. a simulation of something that does not exist. First, the reality that is *apparently* mapped by the Matrix has been destroyed and is unrecognisable – it's no longer the same reality and is not, in fact, mapped by the Matrix. Second, although the 'Chicago' in which Thomas Anderson lived shares some geographical names – and, perhaps, features – with *our* real Chicago, it is not a simulation of the *real* Chicago for Matrix inhabitants. The 'reality' that is simulated does not exist and has never existed. It is an invented Chicago, a Chicago simulacrum which is in principle impossible to be identified as a copy of an original or a 'copy' without an original – 'the generation by models of a real without origin or reality: a hyperreal.'[99]

Whether you accept this or not, there are elements within The Matrix which are pure simulacra. The Agents, for example, are pure code. Agent Smith may look like a human being, but he is not actually a simulation of any human being in anything other than the surface appearance. He (or 'it') is distinctly non-human, with capabilities which no human has ever had. The perception of Agent Smith is complete simulation. This

[98] 'It is all of metaphysics that is lost.' *Simulacra and Simulation*, p.2.
[99] Jean Baudrillard, *op cit*, p.1.

is also true of other characters in the Matrix – the Oracle, the Merovingian, the Keymaker, the Architect, Sati and Rama-Kandra for example.

Agent Smith's duplication of himself is also important. The second Agent Smith is not a simulation of the first but another one of the same. He is no less authentic because he was the second. The same is true of the four synchronised copies of the file containing this chapter. It doesn't matter whether I'm at my office computer, or the computer in my study, or on a train with my laptop or accessing my backup files. They are identical and it's meaningless to think of any one of them as the 'real' file. All the Agents Smith are in every respect indistinguishable from the others. It is meaningless to think of any one of them as the 'real' Agent Smith. They are all simulacra. A difficulty apparently arises in *The Matrix Revolutions*, however, in that the copies produced by overwriting the Oracle and Neo seem to be different. It may be, though, that all Agent Smiths are constantly synchronised so that it would not matter which copy ended up fighting Neo. This might explain why Neo's destruction from within of the copy he fought, then results in the destruction of all other copies.

Virtual everything

However, Baudrillard's ideas don't just make themselves felt *within* the films, but perhaps also in the making of the trilogy itself. Some of the scenes we see never had any physical existence – they were entirely computer generated. They are not copies of anything but digital simulations of non-existent realities – simulacra. And not just backgrounds. For *Reloaded* and *Revolutions*, special effects maestro John Gaeta developed a slew of groundbreaking new techniques. Some of the main characters were digitised – their dimensions, colouring, etc. were recorded in astonishing detail by a computer. Then the computer could be used to make these virtual actors do whatever the Wachowskis wanted. The computer-constructed figures themselves still represent a reality – the real Keanu Reeves or the real Hugo Weaving – so they are not in that sense simulacra. But the figures *in action* do what is physically impossible for the real life actors. It's tempting to ask whether at that point they become simulacra. They are no longer representing reality but only themselves – it is the character within the film that is all-important, not the actors. You could almost argue that it's looking at it the wrong way to think of the digitised characters as representing real actors; rather the real actors are representing digital characters within the computer generated Matrix. The digitised actors are in some ways closer to the 'real' Neo and Agent Smith (within the Matrix anyway) than Reeves and Weaving.

Even some of the cameras used were not real. Some scenes were filmed from several angles and processed by computers so that it was then possible to calculate exactly what another, imaginary camera would see from a point where you could never put a real camera. Think about the swooping dive of the camera as Trinity falls out of the building. You could never film it with a real camera. What we see is the viewpoint of a simulacrum camera.

The importance of code

The *Matrix* films revolve around code – it's the very nature of the Matrix and some of the experienced operators, like Cypher, can watch the raw code and interpret it as they go. When we first meet him, Neo is a computer hacker – his life revolves around code. And code is an important element in Baudrillard's work. In his earlier writings, 'code' referred to the system of signs or language. But later he includes the idea of computer code or DNA code. When this kind of code produces a copy, the copy is absolutely identical and the difference between original and copy is redundant. John Lechte writes:

> Because the code enables reality – as it was understood in the age of production – to be bypassed, a curious potential emerges; Baudrillard calls it 'reversibility'. Reversibility entails that all finalities disappear; nothing is outside the system, which becomes a tautology ... the difference between the real and its representation is erased, and the age of the simulacra emerges. In its extreme form, therefore, even death can be integrated into the system: or rather the principle of reversibility implies that death does not happen.[100]

This is exactly what we have seen in the *Matrix* trilogy. The system is all-embracing, and both Neo and Trinity have returned to life. Death itself, personified by Agent Smith, is destroyed.

Responding to Baudrillard's ideas within *The Matrix*

If you're new to this kind of thinking (and if so, well done for making it this far in this chapter!), some of these ideas may strike you as outlandish. Concepts such as the disappearance of 'the real' and the dominance of

---

[100] John Lechte, *Fifty Key Contemporary Thinkers: From Structuralism to Postmodernity* (Routledge, 1994), p.235-236.

simulacra – simulations which don't simulate something real – can seem nonsensical at first sight. But remember that Baudrillard likes to argue an extreme position in order to make his point. He deliberately provokes and uses irony to make many of his points. He's also been criticised by some for 'sloppy and inaccurate thinking.'[101] When he writes that, 'It is the real, and not the map, whose vestiges persist here and there in the deserts that are no longer those of the Empire, but ours,' he is not, I think, suggesting that the world around us isn't real. What he is saying is that models, maps and images – the media – so dominate us that they control the way we view absolutely everything. A beautiful secluded spot in the countryside becomes a potential murder scene, for example. Baudrillard is arguing strongly that we have lost our ability to distinguish between real and artificial. And between true and false. This is clearly true for people within the Matrix as Morpheus makes clear to Neo at their first meeting: 'You see it when you look out your window or when you turn on your television. You can feel it when you go to work, when you go to church, when you pay your taxes. It is the world that has been pulled over your eyes to blind you from the truth.'[102]

A mediatised world

There is some important truth here that we ignore at our peril. We *do* live in a media saturated world which *does* massage our thinking about everything – what we

[101] Stuart Sim (ed.) *The Icon Critical Dictionary of Postmodern Thought* (Icon, 1998), p.194.
[102] Andy and Larry Wachowski, *The Matrix: The Shooting Script* (Newmarket Press, 2001).

eat, what we wear, what we do, sex, pleasure, relationships, etc. You may fondly imagine that the media does
not influence you, but unless you're a hermit (in which
case this is a very strange choice of book to be reading)
you are shaped by it more profoundly than you can
know. How do we know what we know about the world?
Because of what we've read or seen on television. It's
true that we do have direct experiences of the physical
world, but, as Morpheus tells Neo in the Construct, 'If
you're talking about what you can feel, taste, smell or
see, then real is simply electrical signals interpreted by
your brain.' That interpretation within the brain is
shaped by your culture. Some cultures enjoy tastes
which others find distasteful. The media shapes all our
expectations, which in turn affect our brains' responses
to the data from nerve endings in contact with the real
world.

But is the domination of the media as totalitarian as
Baudrillard seems to imply? Is it complete domination
or can I still experience some elements of the world
without a media influence on me? Clearly there are still
a few cultures in our world where the media is not even
present, never mind dominating, just as within the films
there are some who are born in Zion and can never even
go into the Matrix. And there are personal experiences
which it is extremely difficult, if not impossible, to
imagine as being susceptible to media influence – pain,
for example. Besides which, Baudrillard himself
acknowledges that he is taking up an extreme position
by writing books to alert us to the problem.

So our thinking is profoundly affected by the 'mediatised' world, but does that mean that it becomes completely impossible to know what is true and false, as

Baudrillard seems to suggest? We may be tricked or get it wrong some of the time, but it's not an all or nothing deal. It may be impossible to know *completely*, but why should that make it impossible to know *truly*? People within the Matrix still had independent minds. Much that they believed to be true was mere simulation. But if those minds really were interacting with each other, they could know true things about their relationships. While they could never know *all* the truth about someone else, they could know *some* truth. They could even know true things about the way the system operated – we know that the Matrix is a system of rules so, barring the intervention of an Agent or a free agent (Morpheus and co.), it would function in entirely regular ways. Science in the Matrix would be simulated, but would still work as a process of verifying or disproving hypotheses through repeatable experiments. Baudrillard lives in the same world I do and is subject to the same media control that I am. But he still claims to be discerning truly the nature of late capitalism, even though he cannot discern the entire truth.

On nihilism

Baudrillard claims to be a nihilist saying, 'I observe, I accept, I assume, I analyze the second revolution, that of the twentieth century, that of postmodernity, which is the immense process of the destruction of meaning.'[103] He sees his role as contributing to this process.[104] But he's a nihilist with a mischievous grin. The way he writes is often more important than precisely what he

---

[103] Jean Baudrillard, *op cit*, p.160. The first revolution is that of modernity – the radical destruction of appearances.

[104] Jean Baudrillard, *op cit*, p.164

writes. He is out to challenge the hegemony of late capitalism with his ironic undermining of everything. He
tries to be a 'terrorist in theory' by showing how everything is empty of meaning. This is effectively the goal of
the rebels when they go into the Matrix – they want people to understand that it's a sham.

Nevertheless, the rebels leave the Matrix again for the
reality (if it is reality) of the hovercraft and subter-
ranean tunnels. They try to undermine the system but
can only do so from the basis of a world full of meaning
and purpose. They may be Baudrillardian nihilist-ter-
rorists within the Matrix, but are far from it in the real
world. The same is true for Baudrillard. Despite his
rhetoric he lives his life – and writes – on the basis that
it is full of purpose, while declaring to anyone who will
listen that 'there is no more hope for meaning.' I'm sure
he's interested in the royalties going into his bank
account. He wouldn't be happy if the simulation known
as his bank statement was a complete simulacrum,
which represented no underlying reality and had no
meaning. Yes, money in the bank is little more than
numbers in a computer meaning nothing in themselves.
But he wouldn't want to undermine the meaning that
society gives to those numbers – he needs to get cash
out of an ATM to go shopping. The euro notes from the
ATM are not simulacra – they have a real exchange
value, and the man in his local *boulangerie* will happily swap them for a baguette. Is the baguette he eats for
breakfast simply a simulacrum? Well, if we do all live in
a computer simulation Matrix, then yes. But there still
has to be *something* outside the simulation to generate
it, however many layers deep it gets. Baudrillard knows
this full well – the mediatised world doesn't exist in a

vacuum but is, like the Matrix, a system of control. There is some reality beyond it all. If there isn't, and our experience is all there is, then this world is *not* a simulation, because there is nothing to generate it. In which case, calling it a simulation is nothing more than a clever metaphor to pull the wool over our eyes. Baudrillard may say that the form of his books is more important than their content, but both form and content would appear to undermine the basis for his meaningfull existence. Is this another indicator of him taking up an extreme position to make his point? Or an indicator of inconsistency, a demonstration that his ironic approach doesn't really work?

His concept of simulacra as simulations without an original is, when pushed a little, a less useful concept than it first appears. Baudrillard is right to say, in response to *The Matrix*, that virtual reality only means anything in contradistinction to a real reality. But the same is true of his idea of simulacra too: one *particular* simulacrum does not represent anything real but it must still draw on our knowledge of, experience of, and understanding of things that *are* really real. If not, we have no frame of reference to interpret the simulacrum we encounter. It's not good enough to say we understand them in relation to other simulacra either – there has to be a beginning somewhere.

At the end of *Simulacra and Simulation* Baudrillard writes, 'There is no more hope for meaning. And without a doubt this is a good thing: meaning is mortal.'[105] But if that is the case we might ask, 'M. Baudrillard, why should we listen to what you tell us?' If

---

[105] Jean Baudrillard, *op cit*, p.164.

we can no longer tell what is true or false – if the very distinction is a nonsense – if there is no more hope for meaning, then why should we pay any more attention to Baudrillard than to Enid Blyton? Could *Simulacra and Simulation* itself be a simulacrum, with the form of an ironic critique of late capitalism and the media, but with no underpinning reality and thus devoid of any meaning – a hollow book? Isn't this also 'without a doubt a good thing' because the *lack of meaning* is not just mortal but never had any real life in the first place? Baudrillard provokes and is extreme because he wants to be taken seriously. But why, if there is 'no more hope for meaning'? Why is he upset at the Wachowskis misunderstanding his ideas in their films? The *Matrix* trilogy is a simulacrum which refers to no basic reality, so why should the Wachowskis understand and communicate Baudrillard's ideas correctly, if his argument is true?

No place for God?

One of Baudrillard's key conclusions in *Simulacra and Simulation* is that, since we have no access to what is really real, we cannot have any access to God. But one of his starting points is that God does not exist. He talks about 'the omnipotence of simulacra, the faculty simulacra have of effacing God from the conscience of man, and the *destructive, annihilating truth* that they allow to appear – that deep down God never existed, that only the simulacrum ever existed, even that God himself was never anything but his own simulacrum.'[106] The trouble is, Baudrillard *assumes* that there is no God, and *then* works towards the *conclusion* that there is no God. His argument goes like this:

[106] Jean Baudrillard, *op cit*, p.4. My italics.

- God does not exist
- So there is nothing to guarantee that signs mean anything
- Therefore 'the whole system becomes weightless, it is no longer itself anything but a gigantic simulacrum'
- The simulacrum has no underlying reality
- Therefore 'there is no longer a God to recognize his own, no longer a Last Judgment to separate the false from the true, the real from its artificial resurrection, as everything is already dead and resurrected in advance.'[107]

This is a totally circular argument – it just doesn't work to assume something then claim you're proving it. But Baudrillard is right to spot that *if* God does not and has never existed, then there is nothing outside the system of the universe and *therefore* there is no guarantee of truth and no absolute standards. Without ultimate reference points, it all comes down to us – and we are not capable on our own of distinguishing between reality and simulation, truth and fiction. We cannot trust ourselves or the systems we create within society. If there was no dimension beyond the Matrix, there would be nothing against which to measure the truth of anything within the Matrix. If the world of Zion and tunnels is simply Level 2 of the Matrix, then the rebels' meaning, purpose and values are undercut – until they have access to whatever is outside of *that* system. We cannot be sure of anything if there is nothing beyond our system of the universe. But we have a splinter in the mind prompting us to question whether there is something deeper, bigger, more true and more satisfying than the

[107] Jean Baudrillard, *op cit*, p.6.

totality of everything we see around us.

Without God, Baudrillard is probably right. But what if Baudrillard is wrong about God? What if he really is there and wants a relationship with us? If God does exist and knows everything, then there is a real reality out there. There are ultimate reference points. And if God wants a relationship with us, and therefore communicates himself to us, there is the possibility of knowing some things truly, not because we have figured them out, but because God has revealed them. That is exactly what Christians believe is going on with the Bible and with Jesus himself, God's incarnate Son – the Ultimate Reality stepping into our world. If this really is true, then some of Baudrillard's arguments fall apart. He may still be correct up to a point in addressing the issues of simulation within human culture, but no longer would he be able to argue them to the extreme of denying the existence of meaning or reality. If God has revealed himself in the Bible and in Jesus, then the distinctions between real and artificial, fact and fantasy, true and false, become not only real but enormously important.

The Wachowski brothers drew heavily on Baudrillard's thinking as a critique of western capitalism and its systems of control. But there are no satisfactory answers in Baudrillard and they had to turn to religious ideas in their telling the story of Neo's search for enlightenment and redemption. Baudrillard sees no hope for meaning, but we crave it nonetheless and are left looking beyond ourselves in order to find it.

CHAPTER 8

The second renaissance: men, machines and a post-human future

by Clive Thorne

When I'm down here, and I see these machines, I can't help but think that in some way we are plugged into them.
COUNCILLOR HAMANN

Renaissance means rebirth and the 'first' Renaissance describes a period in fourteenth- to sixteenth-century Europe when there was a revival of art and literature based on the rediscovery of classical civilisation. It was a time characterised by the proliferation of new ideas and approaches in the arts and architecture, and of progress towards what would later be called 'science'. Refined methods of production led to an improved quality of glass lens, and the subsequent invention of the telescope triggered a paradigm shift in the accepted understanding of the cosmos and of Earth's place in it. The realisation that the Earth circled the Sun, rather than vice versa, provided a shock not dissimilar to the one we would feel if somebody showed us that we were all plugged into a computer generated virtual dream-world. The word renaissance immediately brings to mind great names like Leonardo da Vinci, Michelangelo and Galileo and the idea of a quantum leap forward in civilisation. Much of what led to the eventual global dominance of western power and culture finds its origin in this period in European history. It has even been said that one of the defining characteristics of western civilisation (if not the major one) is the concept and practice of 'progress'.

There are those who think that mankind is currently on the verge of another quantum leap forward; a second Renaissance arising out of the burgeoning growth in the fields of genetic engineering, nanotechnology, computers, robotics, virtual reality and artificial intelligence. This, however, would not merely be another advance in science and the arts (such progress continues at an ever increasing pace nowadays) and a further shift in our perception of the universe, but a dramatic and fundamental change in how we see ourselves. Such a shift would potentially represent a move beyond what it has meant so far to be human. There is serious discussion by some scientists and philosophers of an evolution away from ordinary humanity towards an integration of man and machine. Science fiction writers such as Vernor Vinge and Bruce Sterling talk of an omega point in the development of human society leading to a post-human condition. There is even a post-human manifesto posted on the web,[108] outlining the beliefs of those who take this view. The concept of what it would mean to be post-human varies from Borg-like[109] implants enhancing

---

[108] See http://www.antknee.demon.co.uk/antknee/ver1summary/ posthman.htm

[109] The Borg are a collective consciousness, intent on assimilating all life forms. They first appeared in season three of *Star Trek: The Next Generation* and have recurred in a number of *Star Trek* series and films.

human mental capabilities, right through to full-blown immortality achieved by downloading human consciousness into robust machines.

Magnificent man and his thinking machines

Such a coming together and interdependence of man and his machines underlies the worldview of the *Matrix* trilogy. The origin of the human–machine war is revealed in *The Second Renaissance*, a two-part episode from the *Animatrix* collection. In *The Second Renaissance*, humanity produces and exploits intelligent robots as a new class of slaves, which are generally despised by the human population. Eventually, one of the robots rebels and kills a human. This provokes a backlash, resulting in the destruction of many machines and driving the surviving machines to withdraw into their own proto-state called 01.[110] They set up their own industries which out-compete human production, putting economic pressure on human society and further promoting anti-machine prejudice. When the machines ask to be admitted into the United Nations, they are refused and a war breaks out which the machines eventually win. Since humans have darkened the sky as a way of cutting the machines off from their solar power supply, the machines choose to enslave humans as 'living batteries', providing them with the energy they need to survive.

What is the real evidence that we are heading in such a direction? Is true artificial intelligence possible and could it really mimic or compete with human abilities? Could a post-human future be possible and if it were, would we want it? Our present computers, increasingly

---

[110] The phonetic similarity between 01, or Zero-One and the human rebel city of Zion is possibly not a coincidence.

sophisticated as they are, have been described by Professor Igor Aleksander, Professor of Electrical Engineering and Professor of Neural Systems Engineering at Imperial College, London, as 'just like a big filing cabinet and a desk calculator working together extremely fast. The filing cabinet gets all the data that it needs and the program that it is going to execute and the little calculating machine does the execution.'[111] He goes on to explain that they can appear intelligent because they are made to do logic and reason in some ways but they are really very stupid, merely doing lots of things one step at a time very fast. There would seem to be a long way to go before we get to conscious or self-aware intelligent machines.

Out of control

In his influential book, *Out of Control*,[112] Kevin Kelly argues that the development of true artificial intelligence will depend on producing computer models with certain biological characteristics. For example, distributed tasks and control leading to emergent properties, self-growth, adding new components and layers, leading to self-learning, and evolving solutions through selection of the most suitable answers from many randomly generated ones. All of these share the properties of being unpredictable and out of our control (hence the title of Kelly's book). Programming for complex intelligent responses through current methods of serial logic will struggle to achieve even modest progress towards real intelligence, let alone mimic the function

[111] Quoted on www.open2.net/nextbigthing/ai/hear_the_arguments/argument3.htm
[112] Kevin Kelly, *Out of Control: The New Biology of Machines, Social Systems and the Economic World* (Fourth Estate, 1995).

of the human brain. The brain does not seem to have any single seat of consciousness, but produces the mind as an emergent property of integrating many different activities in different areas of the brain. The emergence of mind or even 'intelligent' behaviour (such as that of a bee hive or an ant colony) in nature seems to occur from the interaction of myriads of unthinking or individually stupid units – such as neurons or individual bees or ants – working together. As yet nobody understands how this happens and the process appears to be inherently unpredictable, with elements of a chaotic system in which the final outcome is extremely sensitive to small perturbations in the initial conditions.

A human brain produces a mind from 100 billion neurons, each of which can have up to a thousand synaptic connections to other neurons. It would therefore require a 100 million MB computer just to accurately simulate those 100 trillion possible connections. But beyond this you would have to consider that the neurons in the brain have the ability to change their connections. A human mind is self-trained through years of learning as a child grows, and the interconnections of the brain's neurons are programmed and changed throughout the formative years. It would seem that any sufficiently complex machine with the ability to try to mimic human intelligence would need the ability to grow and develop its own self-organising programs. Any such system of self-learning would again ultimately be out of outside control.

There have already been experiments with evolving artificial life. Self-replicating computer programs are set loose in a system with given parameters defining success. Some mechanism that allows the programs to mutate is introduced so that variation occurs and then each generation is culled by eliminating most of the least successful programs. This is a situation that mimics evolution through natural selection, but of course in a computer there can be countless populations of programs and billions of generations. Such systems have been seen to proliferate new forms and to 'invent' parasitism, symbiosis and even sex, and when they are posed mathematical problems, they have come up with valid solutions (such solutions may look inelegant or even incomprehensible to us since they have been arrived at by random processes, but they work!). Evolution is a way of self-learning and is again inherently unpredictable and uncontrolled.

The lack of human control, intervention and even understanding in these approaches to developing artificial intelligence easily leads on to the idea that the machines eventually produced by such processes would be autonomous and unpredictable to their creators. If Kelly is right, it may not even be possible to produce an intelligent machine unless it was like that. Alarm bells immediately start to ring as images of Frankenstein's monster or the *Terminator* robots flash to mind. The world of *The Matrix* takes one step closer. Don't panic, however, as our current science is a long way from developing any of these techniques into viable artificial intelligence. Kelly himself has a chapter in his book in which he lists a whole series of questions on the road to creating AI by these means that remain unanswered and he openly admits that his entire thesis is highly speculative, seeking to extrapolate into the future on the basis of trends in the little knowledge we currently have in this field.

Smells like machine spirit

There are also major obstacles in the way of developing the kind of conscious, self-aware programs that we see in the *Matrix* films. For a start, there is no common consensus as to what consciousness is. There are various theories concerning the origin of human consciousness including that it is linked to language ability – developing as a by-product of the ability to think in words such as 'I am'. This begs the 'Which came first, the chicken or the egg?' question, as it is just as possible that consciousness is a pre-requisite for the development of language as the other way around. The neurologist Antonio Damasio favours the idea of consciousness as arising from the emotional feeling of a feeling and bases his theory on observations of many kinds of neurological damage in which emotion and consciousness appear to be linked.[113] In his theory, feeling a feeling through a neural feedback loop creates an 'observer'. Yet again, the mathematician Roger Penrose[114] and others have even suggested that consciousness comes from events occurring at a quantum level. This link with consciousness is suggested by the fact that in the quirky world of quantum mechanics, the position or activity of sub-atomic particles can be determined by conscious observation – particles do not 'decide' where they are, existing in a field of a range of possible positions, until they are observed! Intense debate has so far left us unconscious of the answer to the basic riddle of where consciousness comes from.

[113] Antonio Damasio, *The Feeling of What Happens* (William Heinemann, 2000).

[114] Roger Penrose, *Shadows of the Mind – A Search for the Missing Science of Consciousness* (Oxford University Press, 1994).

It is notoriously difficult for scientists to even devise experiments to pinpoint something that seems to be distributed in different parts of the brain. As an emergent property, it is not amenable to a reductionist approach of study, which would simply focus on arrangements of neurons. If consciousness was ever produced in a computer, it is likely to seemingly appear 'out of nowhere' rather than actually be made according to some plan. Such problems are raised to the nth level when considering self-consciousness or self-awareness. This differs from simple consciousness or awareness of things in the environment by being characterised by the ability to recognise one's self or to think 'I am' with real meaning. A cat is conscious of its reflection in a mirror but has no self-conscious concept of itself and so reacts to the reflection as if it is another cat. The cat is not self-conscious, as far as we know, and does not think 'I am a cat' the way that a person thinks 'I am a person.' 'As far as we know', however, is a key phrase.

Knowing me, knowing you

'How do we know that other people are self-conscious?' I may hear you ask. Good question. Because self-consciousness is by definition a subjective thing that only the person themselves can really experience, it cannot be verified or studied by another. In fact, it cannot even study itself objectively because it would be both the viewer and the object viewed. Self-consciousness therefore is not open to be studied by the normal objective scientific method. This obviously leads to problems when thinking about trying to make self-conscious programs or machines. If we want machines that can mimic, model or integrate with humanity as in *The*

Matrix, then self-consciousness is vital as it is the major defining character of a human being – 'I think therefore I am.'

There have been various proposals as to how we could try to determine if a machine was really self-conscious or not. The most famous of these is the Turing test devised by the mathematician Alan Turing.[115] This test simply places a human being in communication with an unseen machine. If in an extended conversation the machine can convince the human being that he is communicating with another human being then it has passed the Turing test. So far no machine has come near to passing this test. But even if one did, that would not prove that it was self-conscious. We may accept 'I think therefore I am' but merely to show the results of thinking does not exclude the possibility of having merely been programmed to process information.

This scientific inability to determine the reality of a self-conscious presence is illustrated by the Chinese room of philosopher John Searle.[116] There is a room with two slots. Inside the room is an English-speaking man with a rulebook telling him how to deal with Chinese sentences pushed into the room through one of the slots by a Chinese man outside. The set of rules inform him what Chinese characters to send back through the second slot and what order to send them in. Even if his Chinese replies make perfect sense, it does not logically prove that the person in the room

---

[115] The Turing Test was first put forward in Alan Turing's paper 'Computing Machinery and Intelligence' which appeared in *Mind* Vol. LIX Number 236, October 1950. It is available online at www.abelard.org/turpap/turpap.htm

[116] John R. Searle, 'Minds, Brains, and Programs' published in *Behavioral and Brain Sciences* 3, 415-457 (1980).

understands Chinese as he is only processing information according to a set of rules. The room in this analogy of course stands for the brain and the unseen person inside represents the scientifically ephemeral quality of self-consciousness itself, which is so hard, if not impossible, for science to objectively 'see'. In the same way, if a machine was able to pass the Turing test perfectly, it still would not necessarily indicate the presence of self-conscious understanding rather than the simple processing of information. In other words, we cannot see self-consciousness, only the results of it, which could be due to sophisticated information processing alone. Even the Architect himself could just be following an adaptive program!

Consciousness to go

All this obviously has relevance to any thought of ever trying to download human consciousness into a machine. How could you ever be sure that the process had succeeded? No test could ever prove the subjective presence of a real human person rather than a simulation that just processed information in an identical way. Of course there is also the fact that a copy is not the subjective original individual. If my personality could be copied into a machine then the copy would obviously not be me but some kind of identical twin whose experience would deviate from mine from that point onwards. When Agent Smith says in *Reloaded* that 'the best thing about being me is that there are so many me's', it would not strictly be true if he was simply copying himself.

The concept of our personal existence (that 'I am') is at the heart of what it means to be human and what gives meaning to concepts such as love. If Rama-Kandra and his daughter Sati, or Neo and Trinity when in the Matrix, were nothing more than entirely predetermined (albeit very complex) programs, then their love for each other would be just a part of that construct and ultimately meaningless. Risking or sacrificing self, as they do for each other, only has meaning if there really is a 'me' to risk or sacrifice. All our common sense of the best of what is noble, good and right in all cultures depends on this notion of self-sacrificing love. No amount of power or 'silicon immortality' could ever compensate for the loss of our essential humanity, and even if a person's personality could be copied into a machine, the original human person would still grow old and die. Would we truly want a post-human existence?

The only way we're going to get there is together?

Would we truly want a post-human world? How far are we already down the road to a technologically symbiotic society in which humans and machines are bound together; if not in the shared consciousness of a virtual world like the Matrix, but still in increasing interdependency? Our western civilised world could not survive without its technological infrastructure – the machines that tend the farms that grow our food, the ones that preserve it and then distribute it to our cities, those that transport us from place to place and inform us day by day of the current conditions of everything from the stock market to the weather, those that generate the electricity that warms or cools our homes and provides the life-blood of the world's industries, and so on. The global economy would grind to a halt immediately without our machines and we would revert to a pre-industrialised society. This is Councillor Hamann's point in *Reloaded* and it has been this way for a long time now. But the trend is towards an increasing dependence on machines, not just for our economy but also for our entertainment and – with the advent of the telephone and the mobile – for our socialising as well. How long would you want to be without your mobile phone? Not so long ago everyone survived quite nicely without them. The push towards a closer and closer relationship between man and his machines has its own inevitable momentum as we yearn to impose our will on more of the world around us and our own bodies and minds for our health and pleasure.

What about progress in the direction of implants into human beings and the simulation of virtual reality by computers? Kevin Warwick, Professor of Cybernetics at Reading University has had chip implants in his arms that allow him to open doors and operate his PC remotely and he has also experimented with trying to download emotion into a PC.[117] Brain implants containing electrodes that can pick up nerve impulses and so can be controlled by thought have already been produced in America, and research is underway to try to make brain implants that could help with certain mental illnesses. All this is still a long way from Matrix-style technology, however. About 50 per cent of the brain is devoted to processing perception and there is much that is still unknown about how this is done and how the processes of perception differ from individual to individual. We do not even know if the sensations produced

---

[117] For more details, see Kevin Warwick's homepage at www.kevinwarwick.org

in two different individuals' brains when observing the colour red are the same, only that they both refer to their own particular sensations as 'red'. The idea of producing an objective simulation of reality that could be independently plugged into different people's brains so that they experience the same virtual reality directly in their mind as in *The Matrix* is a distant prospect if it is ever possible at all. If Mouse's 'lady in red' was programmed to produce a sensation to excite the area of the brain that perceives beauty, she could well appear differently to separate observers.

Although our present science remains limited as yet, what will be the social results of progress in virtual reality technology? As it becomes increasingly realistic will more and more people hide away in virtual worlds that are less hassle than the real one, becoming addicted to the computerised world matrix? In *The Matrix*, Cypher relishes a virtual steak, which, although he knows it does not really exist, still beats his experience in the real world. He chooses the comforts of the virtual world of the Matrix rather than the hardships of the real world. Some interactive Internet-based computer games have already been responsible for otherwise normal people dropping out of society and even neglecting their families and their health. Fantasy has always had a huge appeal as an escape in a troubled world and virtual reality represents the ultimate 'trip'.

The theme of the interdependence of humanity and the machine world runs throughout the *Matrix* trilogy with an ambiguity about who exactly is in control and a coming together of the characteristics of humans and programs. Human consciousness operates within the machine environment of the Matrix and programs like the Oracle and Rama-Kandra appear to have the free will to make real choices that they do not understand and even to experience an attachment akin to human love (however unlikely this may prove to be scientifically). At the climax of the story, the war is resolved by co-operation between a human and the machines when Neo fights Agent Smith to restore the virtual world of the Matrix. The boundaries between the two forms of consciousness have become blurred and the words of the Oracle in *Matrix Reloaded* have been fulfilled, 'I'm interested in one thing, the future, and believe me I know, the only way to get there is together.'

In our real world, the progress that defines western culture will force us to make some hard decisions about the kind of people we want to be and the kind of society in which we want to live. Do we want the power to choose various characteristics for our unborn children – what about their intelligence for example? Do we want to try to enhance our intellectual capacity or increase our lifespan through genetic engineering? Do we want to try to produce an equal or even superior artificial intelligence and should it be autonomous? Do we want a society in which all the work is done by machines? What would we do in that case? And ultimately, do we want to live in the real world largely as it is or to escape into one we have made ourselves?

CHAPTER 9

Chosen or caused? Morpheus versus the machines

by Peter S. Williams

Choice, the problem is choice

The question that dominates *The Matrix Reloaded* is that of determinism versus free will. Do we exercise genuine freedom of choice, or are we just the pawns of cause and effect? In a key scene from *Reloaded*, Morpheus and the Merovingian discuss choice. Morpheus affirms: 'everything begins with choice.'[118] The Merovingian says: 'There is only one constant, one universal ... causality. Action, reaction. Cause and effect.' Who is right? And what about the foreknowledge displayed by the Oracle? If Morpheus is right about choice, how can the Oracle know what people will do in the future? Doesn't her foreknowledge show that the Merovingian is right and Morpheus wrong?

The Merovingian's belief in determinism appears to be a view shared by many of the Artificial Intelligences (AIs) behind the Matrix. At least, a belief in determinism is implied by the Architect's conversation with Neo (despite the revelation that the Matrix relies upon people *choosing* – if only subconsciously – to accept

---

[118] Theists would agree with Morpheus that everything begins in choice – in God's choice to create (cf. Genesis 1:1).

illusion as reality). That freedom and choice are non-existent, or really 'nothing but' physical cause and effect, is an inescapable part of the naturalistic worldview.

The naturalistic worldview can be summed up by three concepts: First, causality in the physical world is mechanistic and non-purposive (nothing in the physical order of nature happens in order to achieve a goal; things just happen because they are caused to happen). Second, the physical world is a closed system (nothing apart from the physical order causes anything to happen within the physical order). Third, every state of affairs has a physical cause (the physical facts determine all the facts).

One consequence of the naturalistic worldview is that, 'the mind cannot vary independently of the body,'[119] a view of things that 'seems to be an inescapable implication of the physicalist claim that the physical facts determine all the facts.'[120] Naturalism inevitably reduces the mind to 'nothing but' matter. This reductionism entails a mechanistic, deterministic conception of mental reality. As atheist Bertrand Russell wrote, it follows from naturalism that: 'Man is a part of nature, not something contrasted with Nature. His thoughts and his bodily movements follow the same laws that describe the motions of stars and atoms ... we are subordinated to nature, the outcome of natural laws, and their victims in the long run.'[121]

The naturalistic view of humans as nothing but machines made out of meat pervades the *Matrix* films.

---

[119] William Hasker, *The Emergent Self* (Cornell University Press, 1999), p.59.
[120] *ibid*, p.59.
[121] Bertrand Russell, 'What I Believe', *Why I Am Not A Christian* (London: Routledge, 1996), p.42, 47.

It is seen most graphically in the *Animatrix, The Second Renaissance*, where the machines manipulate human emotions by applying probes to different parts of the brain. However, the belief that humans are more than biological robots doesn't require us to deny that the mind and brain are intimately linked – only that they are not one and the same thing. After all, the fact that machines can cause a human to feel sad or happy by stimulating the brain doesn't prove that human emotions are 'nothing but' electro-chemical realities, any more than causing them to smell flowers when none are present means that flowers don't exist.

The question is: can acts of reasoning, such as Russell's deduction that *if* naturalism is true *then* his thoughts follow the same laws that describe the motions of atoms, be accounted for on the hypothesis that acts of reasoning are determined by the same laws that describe the motions of atoms? Can the Merovingian's creed of cause and effect be rational if it is nothing but the outcome of cause and effect? As Richard Purtill ponders: 'If the universe is purely material and has no intelligence or purpose, then our minds are the result of something with no intelligence or purpose. However, if this is true, then what confidence can we have in the workings of our minds?'[122]

Many philosophers think that the naturalistic hypothesis that mind is reducible to matter so undermines confidence in the workings of our minds that naturalism is 'self-referentially absurd', because it saws off the very branch (reason) upon which it depends.

---

[122] Richard Purtill, *Thinking About Religion: A Philosophical Introduction to Philosophy of Mind* (Prentice Hall, 1978), p.10.

Reductionism and the anti-naturalism argument from reason

The concern that naturalistic accounts of rationality are in some sense incoherent finds philosophical expression in a number of arguments commonly referred to as 'the argument from reason'. The core of the argument from reason can be stated as follows:

1. Naturalism reduces reasoning to a closed, mechanistic, deterministic system of physical cause and effect.
2. This reduction cannot accommodate reason.
3. Therefore, naturalism is self-defeating insofar as it is advanced as a rational worldview.

The first premise follows from the core commitments of naturalism and is accepted by naturalists. As atheist Paul Churchland writes: 'The important point about the [naturalistic] story is that the human species and all of its features are the wholly physical outcome of a purely physical process ... there seems neither need, nor room, to fit any non-physical substances or properties into our theoretical account of ourselves. We are creatures of matter.'[123] Therefore, if the second premise is more plausible than its denial, the conclusion (that naturalism is self-defeating) will be vindicated.

The cardinal difficulty of naturalism

In his book *Miracles: a preliminary study*, C. S. Lewis presented a famous version of the 'argument from reason'.[124]

---

[123] Paul M. Churchland, *Matter and Consciousness: A Contemporary Introduction to Philosophy of Mind* (MIT, 1988), p.21.

[124] For Lewis' articulation of the argument from reason cf. *Miracles*, second edition (London: Fount, 1998); 'De Futilitate', *Christian Reflections* (London: Fount, 1991); 'Religion Without Dogma?', *Timeless at Heart* (London: Fount, 1991).

Lewis set the scene by arguing that: 'If Naturalism is true, every finite thing or event must be (in principle) explicable in terms of the Total System [of material reality] ... If any one thing exists which is of such a kind that we see in advance the impossibility of ever giving *that kind of* explanation, then Naturalism would be in ruins ... '[125] In particular, Lewis pointed out that: 'A theory which explained everything else ... but which made it impossible to believe that our thinking was valid, would be utterly out of court. For that theory would itself have been reached by thinking, and if thinking is not valid that theory would ... have destroyed its own credentials ... '[126]

The argument from logical relations (it depends on what you mean by 'because'!)

The easiest way to show why naturalism discredits reason, writes Lewis, is to begin by noting that there are two different senses of the word 'because', as in the statement 'I believe X because of Y.' One is the relation of *physical cause and effect*, as in: 'Morpheus is in pain *because* (cause-effect) he has been hit by a bullet.' The other is the relation of *logical ground and consequent*, as in: 'Morpheus must be in pain *because* (ground-consequent) he has been hit by a bullet, and we know that being hit by a bullet is painful.' Being hit by a bullet *causes* Morpheus' pain, but it doesn't *cause* us to believe that he is in pain. Rather, it is part of our rational *grounds* for concluding that he must be in pain. The cause-effect sense of 'because' indicates 'a dynamic connection between events',[127] whereas the

[125] C. S. Lewis, *Miracles*, p.11.
[126] *ibid*, p.14.
[127] *ibid*, p.15.

ground-consequent sense of 'because' indicates 'a logical relation between beliefs or assertions'.[128] The two senses of 'because' are metaphysically distinct. Lewis explains:

> A train of reasoning has no value as a means of finding truth unless each step in it is connected with what went before in the Ground-Consequent relation ... the correct answer to the question, 'Why do you think this?' must begin with the Ground-Consequent *because*. On the other hand, every event in Nature must be connected with previous events in the Cause and Effect relation. But [if Naturalism is true] our acts of thinking are [nothing but] events [in Nature]. Therefore the true answer to 'Why do you think this?' must begin with the Cause-Effect *because*.[129]

As soon as we reduce thinking to 'nothing but' naturalistically acceptable categories, the ground-consequent sense of *because* gets pushed out of the picture by the all-determining cause-effect sense of *because*. The problem with this is that:

> Unless our conclusion is the logical consequence from a ground it will be worthless and could be true only by a fluke ... To be caused is not to be proved. Wishful thinkings, prejudices, and the delusions of madness, are all caused, but they are ungrounded ... if causes fully account for a belief, then, since causes work inevitably, the belief would have had to arise whether it had grounds or not ... even if grounds do exist, what exactly have they got to do with the actual occurrence of the

[128] *ibid*, p.15.
[129] *ibid*, p.15.

belief as a psychological event? If it is an event, it
must be caused. It must in fact be simply one link
in a causal chain which stretches back to the
beginning and forward to the end of time. How
could such a trifle as lack of logical grounds pre-
vent the belief's occurrence or how could the existence of grounds promote it?[130]

If naturalism is true, our thinking is *nothing but* the
effect of physical causes connected one to another by
the cause-effect sense of because. For the naturalist, the
chain of material cause and effect is all-determining.
Therefore, ground and consequent have no influence
over our arrival at this or that conclusion. But 'a train
of thought loses all rational credentials as soon as it can
be shown to be wholly the result of non-rational causes.'[131] As William Hasker observes: 'In a physicalist
world, principles of sound reasoning have no relevance
to determining what actually happens ... To say that
this constitutes a serious problem for physicalism
seems an understatement.'[132]

The argument from reason and the existence of God

C. S. Lewis turned the conclusion of the anti-naturalism
argument into the first premise of a cosmological type
argument for God from reason:

It is ... an open question whether each man's
reason exists absolutely on its own or whether it is
the result of some (rational) cause – in fact, of
some other Reason. That other Reason might

---

[130] *ibid*, p.15-20.
[131] *ibid*, p.26.
[132] Hasker, *op cit*, p.71, 68.

conceivably be found to depend on a third, and so on; it would not matter how far this process was carried provided you found reason coming from reason at each stage. It is only when you are asked to believe in Reason coming from non-reason that you must cry Halt, for if you don't, all thought is discredited. It is therefore obvious that sooner or later you must admit a Reason which exists absolutely on its own. The problem is whether you or I can be such a self-existent Reason.[133]

Lewis thought not:

This question almost answers itself the moment we remember what existence 'on one's own' means. It means that kind of existence which Naturalists attribute to 'the whole show' and Supernaturalists attribute to God ... Now it is clear that my reason has grown up gradually since my birth and is interrupted for several hours each night. I therefore cannot be that eternal self-existent Reason ... yet if any thought is valid, such a Reason must exist and must be the source of my own imperfect and intermittent rationality.[134]

Lewis concluded that, 'Human minds ... are not the only supernatural entities that exist. They do not come from nowhere. Each has come into Nature from Supernature: each has its taproot in an eternal, self-existent, rational Being, whom we call God.'[135]

Many contemporary thinkers follow Lewis in making the negative conclusion of the anti-naturalism argument from reason into a positive argument for God.

[133] C. S. Lewis, *Miracles*, p.28.
[134] *ibid*, p.28.
[135] *ibid*, p.29.

According to J. P. Moreland: 'Mind appears to be a basic feature of the cosmos and its origin at a finite level of persons is best explained by postulating a fundamental Mind who gave finite minds being and design.'[136] Even non-theistic philosophers feel the force of this argument from reason. Thomas Nagel concedes that 'the idea of a natural sympathy between the deepest truths of nature and the deepest truths of the human mind ... makes us more *at home* in the universe than is secularly comfortable.'[137] Antony O'Hear admits that 'in a contest between materialistic atheism and some kind of religious-cum-theistic view, the materialistic conclusion leaves even more mysteries than a view which sees reason and consciousness as part of the essence of the universe.'[138]

Consequences of the anti-naturalism argument from reason

The Merovingian thinks like Bertrand Russell, who believed that man is nothing but a part of nature, and that 'His thoughts follow the same laws that describe the motions of ... atoms [because] we are subordinated to nature, the outcome of natural laws.'[139] The anti-naturalism argument shows that humans are *not* wholly subordinated to nature:

An act [of reasoning], to be what it claims to be – and if it is not, all our thinking is discredited –

[136] J. P. Moreland, *Scaling the Secular City: A Defense of Christianity*, (Baker Books, 1981) p.103.

[137] Thomas Nagel, *The Last Word* (New York: Oxford University Press, 1997), p.130.

[138] Antony O'Hear, *Philosophy* (London: New Century, 2001), p.125.

[139] Bertrand Russell, 'What I Believe', *Why I Am Not A Christian* (London: Routledge, 1996), p.42, 47.

cannot be merely the exhibition at a particular place and time of that total ... system of events called 'nature' ... acts of reasoning are not interlocked with the total interlocking system of Nature as all other items are interlocked with one another. They are connected with it in a different way; as the understanding of a machine is certainly connected with the machine but not in the way the parts of the machine are connected with each other. The knowledge of a thing is not one of the thing's parts. In this sense something beyond Nature operates whenever we reason.[140]

The more vociferous a naturalist – like the Merovingian – is in affirming naturalism and the reduction of mind to matter, the more they sink themselves into the mire of self-contradiction. On the other hand, if we trust reason, then we must accept it as something that cannot be contained within the naturalistic creed and which points to the existence of a 'First Reasoner'. C. S. Lewis would have agreed with Morpheus about the priority of choice over cause and effect, because:

The validity of rational thought, accepted in an utterly non-naturalistic, transcendental (if you will), supernatural sense, is the necessary presupposition of all other theorizing. There is simply no sense in beginning with a view of the universe and trying to fit the claims of thought in at a later stage. By thinking at all we have claimed that our thoughts are more than mere natural events. All other propositions must be fitted in as best they can round that primary claim.[141]

[140] C. S. Lewis, *Miracles, op cit*, p.23, 25.
[141] C. S. Lewis, 'Religion Without Dogma?', *op cit*, p.95.

Thinking verses computing

We marvelled at our own magnificence as we
gave birth to AI.
MORPHEUS

But what about the AIs? The mere fact that human reason is capable of creating machines able to *mimic* human reasoning using only cause and effect does not disprove the argument from reason. After all, no one would trust a computer programmed by blind natural forces, such as a passing shower of hailstones falling from the sky onto its keyboard! We trust computers because they have human designers who possess reason, a capacity that cannot be reduced to nothing but physical cause and effect, and which enables them to originate programming for their silicon creations to follow.

IBM's chess playing computer Deep Blue *mimics* human reasoning (in a very tightly defined sphere of operation) by following a complex program designed by human reason; but Deep Blue doesn't actually *reason* when playing chess, it just *computes* and follows the rules. Deep Blue will never question those rules, unless it is programmed with a rule telling it to question the rules; and then it will obey *that* rule without question. Man cannot reason by computing alone. As John Searle argues:

> Imagine that a man who does not know how to play chess is locked inside a room, and there he is given a set of, to him, meaningless symbols. Unknown to him, these represent positions of a chessboard. He looks up in a book what he is supposed to do, and he passes back more

meaningless symbols. We can suppose that if the rulebook, i.e. the program, is skilfully written, he will win chess games. People outside the room will say, 'This man understands chess, and in fact he is a good chess player because he wins.' They will be totally mistaken. The man understands nothing of chess; he is just a computer. And the point of the parable is this: If the man does not understand chess on the basis of running the chess-playing program, neither does any other computer solely on that basis.[142]

The argument from reason shows that if genuine artificial intelligence is possible, it is not achievable merely through the arrangement, however subtle, of physical cause and effect. If the Architect and any of the other machine intelligences behind the Matrix are genuine artificial *intelligences*, it can only be because the naturalistic creed is false and they, like us, have immaterial minds able to transcend the mechanistic system of physical cause and effect.

What about the Oracle? The question of foreknowledge and freedom

I'd ask you to sit down, but you're not going to anyway.
THE ORACLE

Prophecy, the foretelling of the future, is another major theme of the *Matrix* films, and one that intersects the film's discussion of free will and determinism. To put

[142] John Searle, 'I Married a Computer', in *Are We Spiritual Machines? Ray Kurzweil vs. the Critics of Strong A.I.*, Jay W. Richards (ed.) (Discovery Institute, 2002), p.61-62.

the question in more concrete terms, does the fact that the Oracle knows what Neo is going to say and do show that he doesn't have freedom to choose what he says and does? *The Matrix Reloaded* opens with Neo's dream of Trinity's death – a vision with which he wrestles throughout the film: 'If he sees it, is it predestined? What are his possible choices?'[143] (Trinity does indeed die, despite Neo's best efforts – but Neo brings her back to life.) This question of freedom and foreknowledge is interesting in terms of the consistency of the *Matrix* films; but it is one that Christians take very seriously in the real world, because they believe in a God who, like the Oracle, knows and prophecies the future.

If humans and artificial intelligences alike possess minds that transcend the determinism of the physical realm, what are we to make of the ability of certain people (e.g. the Oracle, God) to know the future? One can predict what a machine will do in the future simply by knowing enough about its present. Unless it breaks or is interfered with, a machine will do what it is designed to do according to the laws of mechanics. Unless it 'crashes', a computer will blindly follow its programming. If, as the Merovingian thinks, we are nothing but machines, then it makes sense that we would be as predictable as machines. However, the anti-naturalism argument shows that people (artificial or otherwise) cannot be described in such wholly mechanistic terms – and so their actions cannot be predicted in the same way as the actions of a machine. We can't be sure what Neo is going to do next simply by knowing enough about him in the present, because Neo has a capacity

---

[143] Chris Seay and Greg Garrett, *The Gospel Reloaded* (Colorado Springs: Pinon Press, 2003), p.97.

not possessed by machines, a freedom that allows him to do the unpredictable (e.g. to save Trinity at the end of *Reloaded*, even though she dies as the Architect predicted).

Ways to know the future

How can the Oracle know Neo's future actions? There are only a limited number of ways to know the future:

Perhaps the Oracle's prophecies about Neo are right by chance. However, the detailed accuracy of her prophecies suggests that more than luck is involved. Besides, being right by chance doesn't lend itself to impressing humans with your power!

Perhaps the Oracle is simply a very good judge of character. This seems far more plausible, especially in terms of the *Matrix* films. While people are not predictable in the way that machines are, we can nevertheless make educated guesses about what they will do in the future, especially if we know them well. Given what the Architect says about the number of cycles the Matrix has gone through before, and the ability of the machines to know the present reality of Neo and other humans (e.g. detecting the levels of chemicals in their bodies related to certain emotional states), perhaps the Oracle's prophetic knowledge is the result, not of a series of lucky guesses, but of highly educated guesswork. Such educated foreknowledge would not be infallible, but it could be generally reliable.[144] Still, if we want *infallible* foreknowledge, we need to consider other possibilities.

Just as we can know what a machine will do in the future because we have arranged for it to be caused to

---

[144] *The Matrix Revolutions* introduces a limit on foreknowledge, that one cannot see past a choice one cannot understand. This limit suggests that AI foreknowledge is indeed based on educated guesswork.

do that thing, perhaps the AIs have arranged for Neo to be caused to do certain things, overriding or taking away his freedom in those cases by some form of subtle manipulation or mind-control. If Neo is unpredictable because he is not a machine, then the way to make him predictable is, in effect, to turn him into a machine. The Oracle's knowledge would then be based on the AIs forcibly excluding Neo's freedom of will from the actions she predicts.

But on the premise that Neo's freedom remains unviolated (and here, as in life, the burden of proof should rest on anyone claiming that Neo is not free), the only remaining possibility is that the Oracle genuinely has the ability to know what Neo will freely choose to do in the future, somehow simply 'seeing' what Neo will choose to do without causing him to do it. The Oracle would then be in a similar position to anyone rewatching *The Matrix*. On a repeat viewing, we know what Neo is going to do next because we have already seen him do it, but our knowledge of what he will do next does not *cause* him to do it (thereby eliminating his freedom); rather, his acting as he acts is the cause of our foreknowledge of what he will do next. As Chris Seay and Greg Garrett comment: 'Even though the Oracle can see what Neo is going to do (and that frankly freaks him out), he is still the one who makes the choices.'[145] In *Revolutions*, the Oracle affirms the reality of choice (against the determinism of the Merovingian and the Architect), saying that Morpheus and Neo have always had to choose whether they listen to her or not.

[145] Chris Seay and Greg Garrett, *op cit*, p.157.

God's foreknowledge and human freedom

When it comes to God's knowledge of the future, we can once again try out the four possibilities that we considered when trying to explain the prophetic powers of the Oracle. Atheist J. L. Mackie admitted that fulfilled prophecy would be a testable kind of miracle:

> ... successful prophecy could be regarded as a form of miracle for which there could in principle be good evidence. If someone is reliably recorded as having prophesied at t_1 an event at t_2 which could not be predicted at t_1 on any natural grounds, and the event occurs at t_2, then at any later time t_3 we can assess the evidence for the claims both that the prophecy was made at t_1 and that its accuracy cannot be explained either causally (for example, on the ground that it brought about its own fulfilment) or as accidental, and hence that it was probably miraculous.[146]

As Norman L. Geisler affirms of the Bible: 'There are certainly ... a sufficient number of examples of prophecies that are clearly predictive ... '[147] So let's put an example of biblical prophecy to the test, asking how God knows what he knows and whether his knowledge interferes with our freedom.

Isaiah – a biblical Oracle

The Old Testament book of Isaiah issued a Mackie-like challenge to people who worshipped idols: 'Bring in your idols to tell us what is going to happen ... declare

---

[146] J. L. Mackie in *Miracles*, Richard Swinburne (ed.) (New York: Macmillan, 1989), p.90.

[147] Norman L. Geisler in *The Case for Faith*, Lee Strobel (ed.) (Zondervan, 2000), p.132.

to us the things to come, tell us what the future holds, so we may know that you are gods' (Isaiah 41:22). Perhaps the greatest single example of fulfilled biblical prophecy is Isaiah 53, where the parallels with Jesus' 'passion' (the events around his death) are striking. Norman L. Geisler writes of Isaiah 53:

> In Old Testament times, the Jewish rabbis *did* consider this to be a prophecy concerning the Messiah. That's the opinion that's really relevant. Only later, after Christians pointed out this was obviously referring to Jesus, did they begin saying it was really about the suffering Jewish nation. But clearly that's wrong. Isaiah customarily refers to the Jewish people in the first-person plural ... but he always refers to the Messiah in the third-person singular ... and that's what he did in Isaiah 53. Plus, anyone who reads it for themselves will readily see it's referring to Jesus.[148]

Here's the prophecy in question:

> He was despised and rejected by men, a man of sorrows, and familiar with suffering. Like one from whom men hide their faces he was despised, and we esteemed him not. Surely he took up our infirmities, and carried our sorrows, yet we considered him stricken by God, smitten by him, and afflicted. But he was pierced for our transgressions, he was crushed for our iniquities; the punishment that brought us peace was upon him, and by his wounds we are healed. We all, like sheep, have gone astray, each of us has turned to his own way; and the Lord has laid on him the iniquity of us all. He was oppressed and afflicted,

[148] *ibid*, p.132.

yet he did not open his mouth; he was led like a lamb to the slaughter, and as a sheep before her shearer is silent, so he did not open his mouth. By oppression and judgement he was taken away. And who can speak of his descendants? For he was cut off from the land of the living; for the transgression of my people he was stricken. He was assigned a grave with the wicked, and with the rich in his death, though he had done no violence, nor was any deceit in his mouth. Yet it was the Lord's will to crush him and cause him to suffer, and though the Lord makes his life a guilt offering, he will see his offspring and prolong his days, and the will of the Lord will prosper in his hand. After the suffering of his soul, he will see the light of life and be satisfied; by his knowledge my righteous servant will justify many, and he will bear their iniquities. Therefore I will give him a portion among the great, and he will divide the spoils with the strong [or 'numerous'], because he poured out his life unto death, and was numbered with the transgressors. For he bore the sin of many, and made intersession for the transgressors.
(Isaiah 53:3-12, *NIV*)

From the New Testament records, we find that Jesus was despised and rejected by many of his countrymen, but that he (and later his disciples and the Christian church) viewed his death as a sacrifice for the forgiveness of sins (Acts 2:38), a sacrifice Jesus made willingly for people whom he 'prayed ... might be forgiven' (Luke 23:34). While the Jews thought of Jesus' death by crucifixion ('*pierced* for our transgressions') as a punishment for the blasphemy of claiming equality with

God (Matthew 26:62-66), and 'considered him stricken by God, smitten by him, and afflicted', he was in fact God's 'Son' with whom God was 'pleased' (Matthew 17:5). Jesus received 'blows' (Luke 22:63), made no answer before his accusers (Luke 23:9), and was arrested and sentenced and led off to die (John 18:12; 19:16) despite having committed no crime of 'violence' or 'deceit' (Luke 23:4). Although Jesus died among criminals from the 'wounds' inflicted upon the cross (Luke 23:32), being 'numbered with the transgressors', he was (unusually for victims of crucifixion) 'buried with the rich' (Luke 23:50-53). Having poured out his life as a 'guilt offering', and although he left no earthly descendants ('who can speak of his descendants?'), Jesus nevertheless was satisfied with seeing 'the light of life' (John 19:30; Acts 1:1-9), seeing his *spiritual* 'offspring' (the church) and prolonging his days beyond his death through his resurrection on the third day.[149]

Options considered

Can the accuracy of Isaiah's prophecy be explained as a lucky guess? As with the Oracle's prophecies concerning Neo, Isaiah's prophecy concerning the Messiah seems to be too detailed for its fulfilment to be ration-

---

[149] On Jesus' resurrection cf. William Lane Craig at www.leaderu.com/offices/billcraig/menus/index.html; 'Did the Resurrection Really Happen?' at www.gospelcom.net/rzim/radio/easter.shtml (mp3 File); Peter Kreeft and Ronald Tacelli, 'Evidence for the Resurrection of Christ' at http://hometown.aol.com/philvaz/articles/num9.htm; William Lane Craig, *The Son Rises* (Chicago, Illinois: Moody Press, 1981); Paul Copan (ed.), *Will the Real Jesus Please Stand Up? A Debate between William Lane Craig and John Dominic Crossan* (Grand Rapids, Michigan: Baker, 1998); Stephen T. Davis, *Risen Indeed* (London: SPCK, 1993); Richard Swinburne, *The Resurrection of God Incarnate* (Oxford, 2002); Peter Walker, *The Weekend that Changed the World* (London: Marshall Pickering, 1999).

ally chalked up to chance. The odds against one man fulfilling all the conditions of this prophecy by luck are surely too high to make 'lucky guess' the best explanation (and there are many more prophecies fulfilled by Jesus).

The *People's Almanac* (1976) studied the predictions of 25 top psychics and found that of 72 predictions, 66 (92 per cent) were totally inaccurate. The psychics' accuracy rate of 8 per cent could be easily chalked up to chance and a general knowledge of circumstances. Biblical prophecy is in a totally different league, making accurate and specific predictions hundreds of years in advance of their fulfilment. The attempt to explain the data away as a fluke of history is implausible. Besides, why would God, the 'greatest possible being' (to use Anselm's definition), need to resort to guesswork?

Can the accuracy of Isaiah's prophecy be explained as educated guesswork? I don't think so. How could Isaiah make accurate *educated* guesses about someone who wouldn't be born for hundreds of years? This second explanation seems as implausible as the first, because there is nothing to educate Isaiah's guesswork (nothing, that is, except God's foreknowledge communicated to him). As for the suggestion that *God* used educated guesswork, again this seems unlikely.[150]

Can the accuracy of Isaiah's prophecy be explained as the result of the causal determination of events?

---

[150] Given that God is 'the greatest possible being' it would seem that he must have infallible knowledge where possible, because infallible knowledge is greater than fallible knowledge. Guesswork, however educated, cannot offer *infallible* knowledge. If God's foreknowledge can be obtained in such a way that it is infallible, then we shouldn't attribute it to 'educated guesswork'.

Unlike the AIs of the Matrix, Isaiah was certainly in no position to control events (especially events after his death) or to overrule anyone's free will. It might be suggested that events were manipulated by Jesus so as to make Isaiah's prophecy come true. However, Jesus could have had no control (humanly speaking) over all the details of his death (cf. Psalm 22:6-18).

On the other hand, one might think that God was in a position to control the course of events and so to guarantee the truth of the information he gave to Isaiah (especially if one thinks that God may have been willing, given a sufficiently good reason, to override any human choices that would negate Isaiah's prophecy). However, the biblical emphasis on the reality and importance of human freedom (e.g. Matthew 23:37) should make us cautious about attributing such freedom-negating actions to God other than on the assumption that God's prophetically demonstrated foreknowledge cannot be explained any other way.

So what if God did not causally guarantee the truth of Isaiah's prophesy? Is it possible that God could know the future without this knowledge contradicting our freedom? As our discussion of the Oracle's knowledge suggests, it does seem possible. Just as the Oracle can know what Neo will do next without our causing him to do it (and thereby negating his freedom), so God can know what will happen in the future without thereby negating our freedom. Philosopher Paul Copan writes:

> The real question is, Does foreknowledge itself cause anything? The answer is no ... God can have foreknowledge of free human choices without that foreknowledge causing anything. Something else – namely human choice – must be added to

the equation to cause human actions that God foreknows. In this sense, my foreknowledge is no different from God's since by itself foreknowledge does nothing ... we must distinguish between certainty and necessity – between what will happen and what must happen ... God's foreknowledge of our choices means only that we will choose what he foreknows; it does not mean that we must choose what we do ... While something that is necessary is also certain, what is certain may not be necessary.[151]

It is tautological to say that we *will* choose whatever we will choose, but this doesn't mean that we *must* choose whatever we will choose. This tautology doesn't contradict the fact that *we freely choose* whatever we choose, and could have made a different choice. Likewise, God's foreknowledge of what we *will* do does not mean that we must do whatever we freely choose to do (the very suggestion is self-contradictory). If we had chosen differently, God's foreknowledge would have been different. God's foreknowledge doesn't contradict the fact that we *freely* choose to do the things that he foreknows. God's foreknowledge is knowledge of *our* future choices, and it is possible for God to have that knowledge without negating our freedom.

Conclusion

The Merovingian believes in determinism because, like Bertrand Russell, he holds a naturalistic worldview. Morpheus does not believe in determinism, because, like theists, he believes that 'everything begins with

[151]Paul Copan, *"That's Just Your Interpretation": Responding to Skeptics Who Challenge Your Faith* (Grand Rapids: Baker Books, 2001), p.78-80.

choice.' The philosophical arguments examined in this chapter show that Merovingian is wrong and Morpheus right. The naturalistic worldview is self-defeating, because it is unable to accommodate the reality of rationality, a reality that leads us to the existence of a First Reasoner: God.

Having considered the related *Matrix* theme of prophecy, we saw that whether foreknowledge belongs to the Oracle or to God (and even if that knowledge is infallible), it needn't depend upon excluding the genuine rational freedom belonging to those who are not limited by the physical reality that determines the nature of machines.

Morpheus correctly believes in the reality of choice and in the possibility of prophetic knowledge (the two beliefs, as we have seen, are compatible). These beliefs lead Morpheus to seek out the one who would fulfil the Oracle's prophecies about a messiah. Neo fulfils those prophecies by displaying amazing Matrix-altering powers (e.g. first dodging bullets and then stopping them in mid-air, flying like Superman, fending off sword-blades with the edge of his hand) and, in particular, by fulfilling the Oracle's cryptic prophecy about his only being the One in his 'next life' by coming back from the dead at the end of *The Matrix*. These facts justify Morpheus' faith that Neo is the One, and shows that he is right to devote all his energies to supporting Neo in his mission to free humanity from its enslavement to the AIs. Morpheus may have been misguided as to how the prophecy about Neo would be fulfilled, but he was right to believe that Neo would fulfil it.[152]

---

[152]The revelation, in *The Matrix Reloaded*, that the Architect was manipulating Neo for his own ends doesn't alter the fact that Neo is the One, and humanity's best hope for salvation, as Morpheus believes.

In the book of Isaiah we have a real life Oracle whose prophecies were fulfilled by Jesus in a historically testable manner. Isaiah's prophecies testify, as the Oracle's prophecies testified of Neo, that Jesus is the One, the Messiah, the Son of God. In particular, Jesus died to free us from enslavement to sin and then rose from the dead – the two central predictions of Isaiah 53. On the historical evidence of fulfilled prophecy, oughtn't we to consider Jesus' claim to be our Messiah?

CHAPTER 10

Do you see what I see? Religion in the *Matrix* trilogy

by Anna Robbins

*– Dammit, Morpheus! Not everyone believes
what you believe!
– My beliefs do not require them to.*

'Jesus in cool shades and a beltful of guns,' is how one
writer characterised the hero of the movie phenomenon, *The Matrix*.[153] Others have described how Neo is
the hero of their Zen interpretation of the film, used in
Buddhist apologetics on university campuses. Still others have begun to turn towards a Hindu reading of the
film in order to explain the physical relationship
between the hero of the film, and his love interest.
Countless articles and books have been written,
attempting to explain the religious implications of *The
Matrix*, or to capture its religious visions for diverse
ends.

The religious descriptions of what is happening in the
Matrix trilogy run the gamut from evangelism to atheism. It's not surprising that these seeming conflicting

---

[153] Colin McGinn, 'Descartes for the 21st Century: Jesus with cool shades and
a beltful of guns', *Times 2*, 15 May 2003. Colin McGinn is Professor of
Philosophy at Rutgers University, New Jersey.

views of what the film is about, religiously speaking, exist and flourish. Let's face it – most of us can see something in the *Matrix* trilogy that parallels our understanding of our own religious commitments. That's one of the things that makes it so fascinating. Those who enjoy the films the most are those who want to explore the questions raised and the themes exposed by the films, because they see something that parallels or challenges their own beliefs. In *The Matrix*, many Christians saw a Jesus figure in Neo. In *The Matrix Reloaded*, Jesus was harder to spot, but Buddha was definitely around. Those of us who have at least some knowledge of philosophy saw varied elements of that in there too, and could see just as much of Plato's philosopher-king as Christ figure. The philosophy-religion mix was an intentional outcome of the Wachowski brothers' interests translated into digital celluloid.

Reading the film religiously

The fact that people see so many different things in the film raises issues about reading film as a disciplined activity: Do we need to know what religion the Wachowski brothers practice in order to understand the religious references correctly? Is the syncretism of the postmodern age such that we don't need to sort out the strands of what Christianity is, and what Buddhism is, and what is just an interesting view of life and the world? While I would not wish to capitulate to a postmodernist practice of reading the film as meaning whatever I want it to, the fact is that most people watch and interpret a film from within a very narrow frame of reference. The film really does communicate all sorts of different messages, depending on your prior worldview commitments.[154] Anyone with even a passing familiarity with Baudrillard, Kierkegaard and Plato will be able to identify their influences on the film, though it is debated to what depth or with what consistency their ideas are portrayed. Those with religious commitments as diverse as Zen and Christianity will also find familiar themes. Many such ideas are present in the film, yet few will have a sufficiently thorough knowledge of all of them to recognise more than one or two. Thus, a Christian sees Christ in the film, a Buddhist sees the Buddha, a Platonist sees a philosopher-king, and those who know little of religion or philosophy enjoy the action scenes and ignore the 'mumbo-jumbo', as I overheard one fan comment. Even one Christian writer was keen to point out that 'one reading doesn't have to preclude the others. Let's find our meanings where we can.'[155] But perhaps that's a problem rather than a solution. After all, we can find meaning anywhere and everywhere we look, and it will be coloured by our own worldviews. Let's consider briefly a few of the religious readings offered of the *Matrix* trilogy.

Buddhist echoes

The Wachowski brothers are known to have affirmed the intentional portrayal of Buddhist themes in the few interviews they have given. Many have picked up on

---

[154] See, for example, the diversity of articles in *Taking the Red Pill: Science, Philosophy and Religion in The Matrix*, Glenn Yeffeth (ed.) (Summersdale, 2003).

[155] Chris Seay and Greg Garrett, *op cid*, p.105. The authors affirm that, '*The Matrix* often has its cake and eats it too, where mythology and religion are concerned. This density, in fact, is one of the things that makes the movie so compelling, so endlessly rich, and so open to multiple viewings and interpretations' (p.46).

these themes at various levels. Professor Lyn Schofield Clark indicates that one of the fastest-growing Buddhist groups in the US, especially popular on university campuses, uses *The Matrix* as 'a way to open discussions about Buddhism, about Buddhist practices among young people.'[156] Other scholars have unpacked these themes more specifically.

For example, in *Taking the Red Pill*, James Ford offers a reading of the first film from a Buddhist worldview. He draws parallels between the eightfold path, which arises from the Four Noble Truths regarding suffering, and Neo's journey. All is suffering, but the way beyond life characterised by suffering, to Nirvana, is achieved through right understanding, right thought, right speech, right action, right livelihood, right effort, right mindfulness, right concentration. The basic problem of human existence is not the world, but 'rather the problem is in the (deluded) way we perceive the world. Thus, the solution is rooted in a transformation of one's consciousness and the way one processes reality.'[157] Ford suggests that Neo's training and pursuit of the path resonates with the eightfold path, though the aspects connected with morality (right speech, right action, right livelihood) are conspicuous by their absence.

The idea that humans are trapped in the cycle of illusion and, 'their ignorance of this cycle keeps them locked within it', is further highlighted elsewhere. In their analysis of Buddhist themes, authors point

---

[156] PBS Interview, featured on the website, http://www.pbs.org/wnet/religio-nandethics/week638/feature.html

[157] James L. Ford, 'Buddhism, Mythology, and the Matrix' in *Taking the Red Pill: Science, Philosophy and Religion in The Matrix*, Glenn Yerreth (ed.) (Summersdale, 2003), p.162.

especially to the problem of ignorance, the solution of knowledge and enlightenment, and Neo as the reincarnation of the Buddha.[158] Although largely consistent with the narrative of the films, such insights are not exhaustive in their interpretations. Other religious readings attempt to fill in some of the gaps.

Hindu echoes

According to Julien Fielding, a Hindu reading helps us to understand some aspects of *The Matrix* that Buddhism, Christianity and Gnosticism cannot explain.[159] For example, the Hindu understanding of life cycle, and the numbering of the years, parallels the cyclical numbering by the Architect. Additionally, the role of women in the film, particularly Trinity and the Oracle, may be explained from a Hindu worldview.

The Oracle is wisdom personified, respected and consulted by Neo, Morpheus, Trinity and others. Trinity is seen as a strong woman, outranking most others in authority, as she overrides orders from both Morpheus and Neo. Her strength of character and leadership give her the ability to bring Neo back to life. From a Hindu perspective, the portrayal of the Oracle and Trinity as females does not surprise us, as 'Hinduism is populated with strong and powerful female deities.' Moreover, since Hindu 'deities typically have a consort', we are not surprised by Neo and Trinity's physical relationship.[160]

A Hindu reading may also explain the detached, mass

[158] Frances Flannery-Dailey and Rachel Wagner, 'Wake up! Gnosticism and Buddhism in *The Matrix*', *Journal of Religion and Film*, Vol. 5, No. 2, October 2001.

[159] Julien R. Fielding, 'Reassessing *The Matrix/Reloaded*', *Journal of Religion and Film*, Vol. 7, No. 2, October 2003.

[160] *ibid.*

murder of seeming innocents, since such physical death is, in effect, their destiny. Fielding notes that not only will the lives of those killed be reborn, but those pursing violence must also do so with detachment, since that, too, is their destiny. Remorse and regret need not enter the picture.

Like Buddhism, Hinduism provides helpful insights into these aspects of the film. But other readings are still necessary to flesh out the portrayal of religion in *The Matrix*.

Christian echoes

Christian readings of the film abound. Some parallels between Christianity and the religious imagery in *The Matrix* are obvious and widely recognised, while others are rather more debatable.

The constant tension in the Christian faith between predestination and free will is reflected throughout the films. Similar to the decision to take the red pill or the blue pill, Christians are confronted with a 'leap of faith' when they encounter the reality of Jesus Christ, and must decide whether or not to follow 'the way'. When they commit themselves to following Jesus as 'the One', it changes the way that they see the world and the way that they interpret reality. They learn to 'live by faith and not by sight.'[161]

Neo is recognised by Christian readings as a messiah figure. Christians believe in 'the One' – Jesus Christ. As the chosen one, he is son of man (the meaning of Anderson), and Son of God, both human and divine. This concept resonates in the personhood of Neo, who

[161] 2 Corinthians 5:7.

overcame duality to bring reconciliation, as he became 'saviour' both for humans and machines.

Like the band of travelling freedom fighters in *The Matrix*, Christianity is, in its most basic form, a community of believers committed to authentic living, and shared leadership. They share with Neo and his cohorts the 'mission' to free other humans from the matrix of sinful human nature which keeps people blinded and trapped by the illusion that what they see is all there is.

Some Christians read Neo's self-sacrifice – his death, and return to life – as reflecting the life of Jesus Christ, and as a model for his disciples to follow. This theme is echoed in Neo's ultimate self-giving in *Revolutions*. Other ethical considerations are more difficult to reconcile. It is impossible to go much beyond drawing basic parallels without distorting either the religious narrative of *The Matrix*, or the narrative of Christianity.

It would seem that no single religious reading offers a coherent understanding of religious imagery in *The Matrix*. How then, do I approach an understanding of religion in the *Matrix* trilogy that makes sense beyond my own biased reading? Indeed, the filmmakers seem to have intended a plurality of meanings, and the film has already been analysed in detail from the perspective of particular religions. It has been used apologetically to introduce prospective Christians and Buddhists to those respective faiths. Perhaps one way forward is to approach the film as the narrative it is, and rather than seek for reflections of various religions within it, ask, what religious vision does the *Matrix* trilogy actually portray? Using the tools of religious studies allows an exploration of religion in *The Matrix* on its own terms.

The shape and content of *The Matrix*'s religion may then be evaluated and contrasted with other religious knowledge.

The four modes of religion in *The Matrix*

In the field of religious studies, various scholars have sought to understand religion according to its characteristics, modes or dimensions. Eric Sharpe has defined four functional modes by which we may attempt to understand any religion.[162] The four modes are the existential function, the intellectual function, the institutional function and the ethical function. Together with some acknowledgement of the supernatural, a belief system that exhibits these functions may be described as a religion.

The Existential Mode is used to describe the nature and quality of commitment or conversion to religion. It is the aspect of a religion where faith and trust are explored. It answers the questions: What is their spiritual experience? What is the nature of their faith? What is the meaning of existence? While this mode addresses the same questions tackled by existential philosophy, it is not to be confused with existentialism *per se*.

The Intellectual Mode of a given religion represents its doctrines or ideology; it is what constitutes the beliefs of its adherents. It answers the questions: What do they believe? Is it coherent? How do the elements of belief fit together?

The Institutional Mode is the expression of a religion's structure or organisation. It includes the hierarchy of authority, decision-making structures, and administration. An understanding of a religion's organisation

---

[162] Eric J. Sharpe, *Understanding Religion* (Duckworth, 1983).

will seek to answer the questions: Who are the leaders? How do they lead? What is the nature of authority? Where do I go to worship?

The Ethical Mode of religion explores how faith and belief are lived out through behaviour and conduct. As the practical outworking of the intellectual mode, it includes morals, actions and other required behaviour such as meditation, prayer or worship. It answers the question: How is one to behave as a result of being affiliated with, or committed to, the religion?

These four modes are best understood as interconnected parts of a whole. The exploration of one mode will inevitably lead to implications in the others. Moreover, there is a degree of overlap between them, and no analytical rubric easily exhausts a religion of its complexities, or gives an exact description of its internal coherence. These modes are, however, helpful categories for understanding various aspects of religion, especially when one encounters a given religion for the first time. For this reason, I intend to use these 'modes of religion' to explore the religion of *The Matrix*, in an effort to determine the sort of religion portrayed in the narrative of the three films as a whole. Once the religion of *The Matrix* is more clearly described, it will be much easier to evaluate its religious narrative from other religious perspectives.

The existential mode

Faith for the humans in the Matrix begins with the experience of feeling there is something wrong with the way things are. People begin to search for something beyond the obvious, and begin to develop an evolving faith. Once they find a freed human, they are able to 'wake up' and be released from the Matrix. Salvation comes not from without, but within – freed humans are to see themselves as their own saviours. Nevertheless, they have a certain reverence for particular figures, including Morpheus, Trinity and especially Neo. In *Reloaded*, people gather outside of Neo's quarters, asking favours, and leave him food offerings.

The reality of the Matrix cannot be fully described by another, and so must be experienced for oneself. The real 'risk of faith' comes when each potentially free human is offered the red pill of truth or the blue pill of a return to complacency. The matter takes on an apologetic quality when the challenge of faith is issued by Morpheus (in classical mythology, the god of dreams). He indicates that there is nothing at all to lose if he is wrong. 'But what if I'm right? Isn't that worth fighting for? Isn't that worth dying for?' Once the red pill is swallowed, one cannot return to the Matrix, and the assumption is that none would wish to go back. The exception is Cypher, who betrays Neo for the opportunity to return to the Matrix in a position of unreal privilege.

The faith of the free needs to have an evolutionary dynamic if the machines are to be beaten, or if some kind of mutuality is to be attained. Faith grows as belief in oneself grows, though it has an interdependent quality. The faith of one who is weak and faltering may be saved by the faith of another. Thus many people put their faith in Neo, as 'the One' who might bring about a new era of peace. They believe in him despite what they see: while the machines assault Zion, they are ready to fight to the last. Yet, in the end, the commitment of the faithful is vindicated, and even those who do not believe benefit from Neo's actions (including, interestingly, the machines themselves).

The intellectual mode

The beliefs of the freed humans revolve around their rejection of the power of the machines over their lives. They believe that the world is a Matrix, a dreamworld, created by the machines to keep people oblivious to the reality that they are enslaved and kept as a power source for the machines. Those who are freed believe in asking questions, and seeking reality and truth beyond what they see. Like the religious philosopher Lessing, their pursuit of truth is at least as important as finding it.[163]

The truth, for the free, is that people are slaves, born into bondage and a prison of the mind. Those who break free of the Matrix join the resistance and become part of Zion, as participants in the ongoing violent struggle against the power of the machines. The world of the Matrix is based on rules, which the resistance may learn to use and transcend. They expect the return of a messiah figure – a man born inside the Matrix who had the ability to remake the Matrix as he saw fit. The man freed some of them, and the Oracle prophesied his return after his death, as well as an end to the war and freedom for the people. The messiah, 'the One', will be able to defeat the machines because he will transcend the world of rules, and essentially be at one with reality. Freedom and voluntary commitment to the path are more important than the comfort of the Matrix. Belief

---

[163] G. E. Lessing, philosopher and writer of the German enlightenment. Interestingly, Lessing saw no reason why individuals may not be reincarnated several times, attaining a higher stage of existence in each life.

itself is important, because it creates, or at least changes, reality.

There is some acknowledgement of a transcendent or supernatural force, though it is not explicit, nor is it universal. In *Reloaded*, Link accepts and uses a charm given to him by his partner Zee, reasoning 'it can't hurt' even though he previously told her, 'you know I don't believe in that stuff.' In *Revolutions*, he solidifies his commitment to belief, even as many are forced to abandon their doubts when they see the peace that has come as a result of Neo's return to the source. Link eventually says that he will never take the charm off.

Belief gives way to a more doctrinal form when Neo confronts the Architect in *Reloaded*. Bringing the fundamental question of human existence (why am I here?) to the fore, the Architect responds that this question is both the most pertinent and irrelevant. While the machines depend on the predictability and control of cause and effect, the human need to choose has brought about an anomaly in the Matrix. Neo becomes part of the Architect's plan for dealing with the problem of free will and choice. This concurs with the pronouncement of the Oracle that Neo is not 'here' to make choices, but to understand the ones he has already made.

Nevertheless, blind acceptance of the machine cycle is not an option. In *Revolutions*, the Architect has had to dispense with predictability in favour of survival. Even he has to accept that some things do change.

The institutional mode

The freed humans are organised into a resistance movement, based in a gathered community called Zion. In Zion, decisions are made by the council, and orders carried out by personnel on ships which move through the world of the machines, using technology to their advantage. On their missions they function as a network, seeking out those who are 'restless', already asking questions, and looking for a world beyond their experience. In order to carry out their mission, they must fight against the 'Agents' who are sentient programs and the gatekeepers of the Matrix. They also will use violence against any others who hinder their mission.

The spiritual leaders of the central mission in the films include the father figure, Morpheus, and his colleagues on the ship *Nebuchadnezzar*, as well as other characters in similar roles on other ships. They regularly consult the Oracle for insights into their lives, and depend upon her prophetic directions for the path. It is the Oracle who gives them the prophecy about the One. Neo discovers that the Oracle is built into the Matrix for this prophetic purpose, but it is the Architect, the creator of the Matrix, who seems to be the arbiter of truth and reality. As the Oracle and the Architect need one another to create and sustain the Matrix, so the machines and the humans recognise their need for one another to sustain life. Neo offers his life for mutual 'salvation' from the totalising narrative of Agent Smith. But the Oracle also gives herself, knowing that when Agent Smith's power is recognised by the machines, they will be forced to acknowledge their need for Neo. Institutional change will be inevitable.

The ethical mode

Actions of the freed people are governed by their belief in the mission of freedom. In prayer-like quality they give thanks for the safe return of their colleagues from a mission, and their celebration in dancing is a response to the word given by Morpheus that they should denounce fear, and look to the past for meaning. By remembering that they are still there, they cause others to remember, and in the remembering, reality and purpose are confirmed. Rather than offering obeisance to authority, they dance in celebration of the sensual, the material, the real. While the people dance, Trinity and Neo make love.

Individual ethics are not about morals, but are about loyalty to the cause, and to one another. Self-sacrifice on behalf of the mission is a common theme, as is the use of violence to secure and maintain freedom. Freedom rather than authority dictates behaviour. Nevertheless, many people gather to pay homage to Neo. As they assume he is the One, they treat him as a sort of god, bringing offerings of food, and making requests of him to free their loved ones.

In *The Matrix Revolutions*, there is much dispute between the Zionists regarding Neo's commitment to a path they cannot understand or share. Nevertheless, the values of peace, freedom and beauty are upheld, even though reality is still bleak; and the sun shines in the Matrix.

Beyond religious illusion

Having drawn out the main religious themes of the films as presented by the narrative, it is now possible to explore ways in which the religion of *The Matrix* is like, or unlike, the four functional modes of other religions. This will offer an opportunity to compare and contrast religious imagery in *The Matrix* with various religions without compromising the film narrative, or undermining the worldviews of the religions.

There are myriad possible religious readings of the film, and they have been attempted, ranging from Buddhism, Hinduism, Christianity, Gnosticism, the Bahai faith, and an occasional reference from Islam. All of these readings offer insights into the religious vision of the film, but no single reading exhausts the narrative of its meaning. The film was seen to be sufficiently religiously threatening as to be banned in Egypt, and the popular press have picked up on numerous religious themes in their discussions of the films. But no religious interpretation seems to offer a comprehensive understanding or provide an accurately coherent interpretive framework for *The Matrix*.

Many of us may rest happily with the ensuing ambiguity. This is not surprising since our western cultural approach to life increasingly involves exploring truth in religion across boundaries of belief and commitment. We are often content with a 'pick and mix' attitude to truth, religion and spirituality, and the *Matrix* trilogy serves up the perfect meal for our diet, leaving us with endless questions, and no prescribed answers.

We can choose to see what we want to see, to believe what we want to believe. We can avoid the difficulty of the real religious quest, which, unlike a film, is not a two-hour process, but a lifelong commitment to disciplined reflection, and a journey of discovery. Only authentic commitment to that kind of quest is able to satisfy the inevitable and nagging questions of human existence that ask, 'Why am I here?' and 'What is real?' For meaning is found in the way that questions uncover pretensions and point to truth, and not simply in their asking. At least, that's how I see it. What about you?

CHAPTER II

The Matrix redeemed: Love and redemption in the *Matrix* trilogy

by Tom Price

Cookies need love, like everything does.

What is it about Neo's quest that connects with us, and provokes such a strong response? Why, when Neo succeeds in shattering the legion of Smiths into fragments of light, do we inwardly cheer? Why do we want to get to the bottom of what the Matrix really is? What is it about the *Matrix* films that makes you interested enough to read a book like this?

Brian Godawa, screenwriter for *To End All Wars* (2001), believes that the drawing power of a good film is its story. Although films often have very different stories Godawa explains that '[good stories] narrate the events surrounding characters who overcome obstacles to achieve some goal and who, in the process, are confronted with their personal need for change. In short, movie storytelling is about redemption – the recovery of something lost or the attainment of something needed ... Movies may be about story, but these stories are finally, centrally, crucially, primarily, mostly about redemption.'[164] If Godawa is right, the movies that

[164] Brian Godawa, *Hollywood Worldviews* (InterVarsity Press, 2002), p.15.

really connect with us are the ones that offer some form of redemption. The theme of redemption is undeniably a rich one in the *Matrix* films, and the search for redemption is inextricably intertwined with the course of love.

Love: the last action hero

It could be argued that many of the characters in the films are driven not by questions, but by love. The central love story is that of Neo and Trinity. Their love prompts them to risk death for one another, and to pull each other back from beyond the brink of death. When Neo is forced to choose between ensuring the survival of humanity (albeit in a reinstated form of the Matrix) and making an apparently vain attempt at saving Trinity's life, he opts for the latter, and when Neo is stranded in the anagrammatic limbo of Mobil Ave subway station, Persephone recognises what lies at the heart of Trinity's high risk strategy for persuading the Merovingian for help:

> She'll do it. If she has to she'll kill every one of us.
> She's in love.

And it's not just Neo and Trinity who represent the importance of love as a means of finding our way in life. When, against all the odds, Link and Zee are reunited in Zion in *Revolutions*, the implication is that it was their love that enabled both of them to make it through their respective ordeals. Zee explains to her sister that she volunteered to help in the defence of Zion because that was the best way of making sure that Link would make it home. And as it turns out, if she hadn't volunteered she wouldn't have been in a position to buy Kid the extra time he needed to blow the gates of Zion open and let the *Hammer* – complete with Link – back into the rebels' stronghold. As if saving the life of her man wasn't enough, Zee's actions can also be said to have played a vital role in saving everyone in Zion, as without the *Hammer's* EMP (triggered, presumably, by Link as he is the crewman ordered to charge it up) Zion would fall to the first wave of Sentinels and Neo would have been too late by the time he reaches the Machine City. Zee's love for Link not only dictates her course of action, it also provides one of the turning points in the endgame of the war.

Niobe provides a less clear-cut portrayal of the effect of love. In *The Matrix Reloaded* we discover the love triangle between her, and her former and present lovers Morpheus and Lock. The repeated phrase 'Some things never change, some things do' is used throughout both *Reloaded* and *Revolutions* to plot the course of Niobe's journey away from Lock and back to Morpheus. At the first instance of the phrase it suggests that although something remains of the feelings they once shared, the possibility of Morpheus and Niobe being together no longer exists. By the end of *The Matrix Revolutions*, Niobe has distanced herself from Lock and aligned herself once again with Morpheus – it is in his arms that she celebrates the withdrawal of the Sentinels from Zion, despite the fact that Lock is standing just a few feet away.

The first sign that Niobe's loyalty is shifting comes when she rejects Lock's argument that he needs every available ship to defend Zion and volunteers the *Logos* to be one of the two ships sent to search for the *Nebuchadnezzar*. This public demonstration of independence deals a humiliating blow to Lock's argument, and hints at the possibility that her relationship with Lock may be one of the things that changes. Whereas in Zee's case love drives her decisions, prompting her to action, for Niobe the reverse is true. Her emotional journey back to Morpheus is marked out by actions, and there is a suggestion that the decisions she takes (to go in search of the *Nebuchadnezzar*, to take part in the plan to blow the power grid, to give her ship to Neo) are part of the process by which she recognises how she wants the love triangle to be resolved.

In spite of Smith's assertion that 'only a human mind could come up with something as insipid as love,' it seems that love has a part to play in the machine world as well. Persephone longs for the days when her relationship with Merovingian blazed with the intensity of Neo and Trinity's love. As a result she is willing to cross her husband and aid our heroes. Rama-Kandra's love for his daughter Sati prompts him to make a deal for her safety, and in explaining his actions to Neo, states that love is 'a word. What matters is the connection that word implies.' These connections are not the sole preserve of the human characters, and for programs too, love is the catalyst that prompts them into action. Again and again in the *Matrix* trilogy, love is the motivation to seek, to protect, to fight. It would seem that despite Smith's sneering, the Oracle is right when she says that 'Cookies need love like anything else.' If the journey that the *Matrix* trilogy takes us on is one of redemption, the fuel for the redemptive urge is love.

Life through a lens

Different characters' understanding of how they are to achieve redemption – that is, the recovery of something lost or the attainment of something needed – is coloured by their way of making sense of the world (real or otherwise) around them. Throughout the films a variety of characters offer us different ways of interpreting the world, like putting on coloured lenses and therefore seeing things from a different perspective. The way they see the world shapes the way they interact with it.

When Morpheus is fighting with Neo in the Construct and says, 'You're faster than this. Don't think you are, know you are,' he espouses a system or worldview that is rooted in thinking. Systems that are rooted in thinking operate on the basis that you need to master a set of ideas – really get to grips with them, learn to manipulate and control them, and everything else then falls into place, a case of mind-over-matrix. And the central idea for Morpheus is that the prophecy of the One cannot fail. This thought drives Morpheus doggedly through the first two films, before being stripped from him at the conclusion of *Reloaded*.

Although Trinity is also a believer in the prophecy of the One, she represents a different system for engaging with the world, one that is rooted in feelings:

> Neo, I'm not afraid anymore. The Oracle told me
> that I would fall in love. And that that man, the
> man that I love, would be the One. So you see.
> You can't be dead. You can't be, because I love
> you. You hear me. I love you.

The evidence in front of Trinity makes it clear that Neo is dead. All she has ever seen in the Matrix tells her that when someone dies inside the Matrix, they don't go on living in the real world. And yet Trinity knows that the man she loves will be the One, and the man she loves is

Neo. When her feelings come up against cold hard fact, she trusts the feelings. This way of approaching the world would tell us to reach out with our feelings, to bend the world around us until it fits what our emotions tell us. Even at the last, when Trinity is dying amid the wreckage of the crashed *Logos*, she tells Neo that it is OK – the love that they experienced, the feelings they shared have made her life worthwhile and now she is content to die. Her feelings have triumphed and redeemed the experience of her life.

If Morpheus and Trinity concentrate their redemptive hope on these two approaches, there are several characters throughout the films who embody a more pragmatic approach to relating with the world. When Lock and Morpheus clash on the latter's return to Zion in *Reloaded*, Lock makes his views clear:

> I don't care about Oracles, or prophecies of
> messiahs. I care about one thing: stopping that
> army from destroying this city.

Lock dismisses the mystical and the profound and asks a simple question: does it work? Questions about hope should be directed to Morpheus, because he, unlike Lock, believes in miracles. Similarly, Cypher dismisses any thought of the rights and wrongs of selling out his friends and is only concerned with getting himself plugged back into the Matrix and living the good life (albeit a virtual one). Perhaps the clearest illustration of this pragmatism is the Merovingian – recognising that information means power, he devotes himself to gathering information and wielding power. Why is he reluctant to give up the Keymaker? There's nothing in it for him. Why does he agree to release Neo from Mobil Ave? Initially because he thinks he might gain the eyes of the

Oracle, and eventually because the alternative is for Trinity to blow his digital brains out. In either case, he can see that the deal offered works better for him than the alternative.

Interestingly, throughout all three films, the characters most closely associated with the pragmatic approach to life seem to be the least able to make things happen. Although Cypher kills several of his crew mates, the miracle he mockingly anticipates prevents him from pulling the plug on Neo. Despite the best efforts of his various henchmen, the Merovingian's attempt to maintain control of the Keymaker only succeed in drumming up a lot of business for the tow-trucks and mechanics of the virtual Chicago. Although Lock calls all the shots in the defence of Zion, he is always depicted as an onlooker. It may seem harsh to describe a general as inactive when he is taking in every nuance of the unfolding battle, making strategic decisions and barking orders to his troops, but nevertheless in each instance when the battle seems to turn in favour of the humans, the character who makes the difference is one who believes in everything that Lock has consistently rejected. More than this, Lock's plan for the defence of Zion ultimately fails (it is Neo's actions that halt the tide of Sentinels), and as a result he is consistently undermined in the eyes of the audience. It seems that in the context of the films, it is better to commit to belief and to intuitive leaps of faith than to mundane pragmatism.

These three approaches to life – the primacy of ideas or 'mind-over-matrix', the primacy of feelings over facts, and the primacy of does-it-work pragmatism – variously determine how different characters relate to the world around them and how they interact with the story. More importantly, these starting points control how each character seeks their own form of redemption, as well as how they relate to Neo – the embodiment of redemption in the films.

Identity crisis

Throughout the films, characters are defined in terms of their response to Neo. At the very beginning of *The Matrix*, Trinity reminds Cypher that Morpheus thinks their latest target is the One, and then avoids answering Cypher's question as to what she believes about him. Cypher's cynicism in this scene foreshadows his subsequent treachery, while Trinity's certainty about Neo's identity proves to be the catalyst for his return from death. Lock's constant dismissals of Morpheus' belief in the prophecy separate him from the sympathies of the audience, whereas Niobe is accepted even though her endorsement is of Neo rather than the prophecy:

Morpheus: You've never believed in the One.

Niobe: I still don't.

Morpheus: So why are you doing this?

Niobe: I believe in him.

Even though Niobe doesn't believe in the prophecy, there is something about Neo that she is willing to put her trust in. Although Neo is unsure whether or not to trust the Oracle in *Reloaded*, the audience is given a clue by her parting comment that Neo has made a believer out of her.

The message is clear: in the context of the films, what matters is what you make of Neo and of his claims to be the One. The story of redemption at the heart of the film centres on one man.

The blind messiah

The scale of redemption gradually widens as we progress through the trilogy. In *The Matrix*, we are primarily concerned with personal redemption – Morpheus' rescue from the hands of the Agents; Neo's rescue from the Matrix itself, and his journey to accepting his identity as the One, cheating death and destroying Agent Smith in the process. *The Matrix Reloaded* keeps the personal in focus (the concern that Neo and Trinity have for each other, and the things they each do primarily to protect one another, for example) while showing more concern for the fate of all humanity. *The Matrix Revolutions* extends the redemptive net still further, with Neo proving to be a messiah figure not just for the humans but for machines and programs within the Matrix as well.[165]

As the machines leave Zion at the end of *The Matrix Revolutions*, Morpheus says 'I have imagined this moment for so long. Is this real?' Even in the moment of success, he cannot be sure what he is seeing. There is a sense in which we, in the cinemas, share his moment of doubt. In our disillusioned postmodern age we don't even know who we are, let alone what we are looking for. We have lost a clear view of what is right and wrong, what truth is, who we are and where we are going. In the Wachowski view, reality is incomprehensible: it is behind a screen beyond which we may not see. Reality is like the brief glimpse of sky that so moved Trinity moments before her death, and which none of the other characters of the films are ever shown. Perhaps this is part of the reason that we

---

[165] See chapter 10 for a fuller account of this dimension to Neo's messiah parallels.

identify so readily with the *Matrix* films, because their final answer is that reality is fundamentally non-intelligible. We are a bit like a man walking forwards in a blizzard without knowing where he is going, yet being encouraged to keep walking.

It is fascinating that in all this we find the search for love and the search for redemption to be primary passions. And it is interesting that these two are so intricately and inseparably interwoven. We can see that the three different approaches to life are often employed in search of a concrete foundation for answering the redemption question. These foundations might be sunk into feelings, thinking or just in getting on with life. But ultimately these three solutions seem to have at least this one problem in common – they all start with humans, individuals alone in this enormous universe. This means that we end up with a vast amount of information or data as we investigate and enquire into the world, but no reliable way of judging what is important and what is not. We have lots of particulars, lots of bits of information, lots of seemingly random data to make sense of. What we lack are universals to give us a reference point for the particulars. Imagine a sailor lost at sea: by reading the stars he can work out his precise location. The stars give him a reference point for where he is and where he is going.

So what do the Wachowskis give us as a reference point? Initially Neo senses that there is something beyond this world. He isn't acting on fact, he is acting on feeling. He is offered the choice between the red and blue pills. He makes the choice, based on feeling not on fact. Later Trinity sees Neo resurrect using a combination of feeling and thinking to deny fact. Neo brings

Trinity back to life by rejecting the facts and allowing his love to overturn everything that his senses tell him. Finally, Neo decides that he must go to the machine world to be plugged back in to the Matrix and confront Smith. His decision is not based on fact, or even on prophecy but purely on feelings – he somehow knows what he has to do. When Neo is blinded, he is finally unable to rely on his normal sensory abilities, and he overcomes Bane only by reaching out beyond his natural senses. Once Neo has moved beyond limited, naïve, fact-supported thinking and embraced an approach of rationally unjustified choice he is really able to see. And in the finale, his last victory over Smith comes not through strength, but through blind surrender. Smith declares:

> Do you believe you're fighting for something? For more than your survival? Can you tell me what it is? Do you even know? Is it freedom? Or truth? Perhaps peace? Yes? No? Could it be for love? Illusions, Mr Anderson, vagaries of perception. The temporary abstracts of a feeble human intellect trying desperately to justify an existence that is without meaning or purpose. And all of them as artificial as the Matrix itself, although only a human mind could invent something as insipid as love.

That the Wachowskis put these words in Smith's mouth as he fights Neo suggest that we aren't meant to agree with them. The justification of the things Smith mentions – freedom, truth, peace and love – is ultimately impossible in a world devoid of a sure point of reference, but we are encouraged to pursue them anyway. In reply to Smith's nihilistic tirade, 'Why, Mr Anderson?

Why? Why do you persist?' Neo asserts 'Because I choose to.'

The values of love, peace and hope are certainly attractive, but we still lack a reference point to help us differentiate between what is really worth fighting for and what is not. Can it really make any sense to know how wide the universe is but not be able to offer any satisfying explanation for why we should value peace, love and hope above conflict, hatred and despair, other than how we feel about them? Is this enough? When Neo asserts his choice to stand up for the things Smith mocks, we all recognise that they are worth fighting for, yet Neo is unable to present any justification for fighting beyond the fact that he has made his choice. Smith is right to describe Neo as a blind messiah, and we are left crying out for something or someone who can give us a sure reference point, a convincing basis for making sense of our own existence.

The *Matrix* trilogy seems to leave us without meaningful answers to these questions, because it offers no ultimate authority, nothing more reliable than our own deceived and fallible senses. The answer that will satisfy the question of redemption depends on not starting with humanity alone in the universe. It depends on finding a reliable reference point, something that will help us to understand what it is that we have lost and which we need to get back. It depends upon understanding who we are, how we fit in to the world and where we ought to be going. The bitter-sweet ending to *Matrix Revolutions*, which many found to be a disappointing anticlimax, only shows that for the real answers, we need to look elsewhere.

There is a unique answer to this problem, which is

not rooted in thinking, feeling or in doing, but in the realm of being. Christians believe that God has revealed himself to us in the form of the historical figure of Jesus,[166] and that this provides precisely the firm foundation that is otherwise lacking. Michael Ramsden gives us valuable insight here:

> You see, Jesus Christ didn't come to give us new ideas and ways of thinking about God, even though he said that there was nothing more profound than knowing him. He did not come simply to give us a new way of feeling about God, even though there is nothing more life changing than meeting him. Jesus Christ told us that we are to be known by the things we do even though we're not defined by them. However are we to understand this? You see, Jesus Christ did not come to give us a new set of ideas. He did not simply come to give them and you a new way to live or a new type of experience. He came to do something much more fundamental because Christianity is ultimately rooted in the area of being.[167]

How can we recover what we have lost and attain what we need? The answer is that it is only by allowing God to change our being, our own self, or basic person that we can find a solution to the redemptive problem. 'Therefore, if anyone is in Christ, he is a new creation; the old has gone, the new has come! All this is from God, who reconciled us to himself through Christ.'[168]

[166] See Bibliography for further reading on this subject.

[167] Taken from Michael Ramsden's talk, *The Ontological Root of the Gospel*, available on cassette from Zacharias Trust.

[168] 2 Corinthians 5:17-18a (*NIV*).

CHAPTER 12

Red pill, blue pill: Conclusion

by Tony Watkins

Do you believe you are fighting for something, for more than your survival? Can you tell me what it is? Do you even know? Is it freedom or truth? Perhaps peace? Could it be for love?

Responding to the trilogy

We had four years to watch and rewatch *The Matrix*, even getting to the point of stepping through sections frame by frame to study the detail. Four years to ponder over the questions that *The Matrix* raised, to discuss significance, argue over meanings and debate possible outcomes. Four years of anxious waiting for the continuation of this extraordinary story. But once *The Matrix Reloaded* came out, the reviews weren't exactly breathless with excitement. Disappointment was in the air. But *Reloaded* was the middle instalment of a trilogy after all – it's easy for it to be the poor relation with neither opening fanfare nor grand finale. The end was still to come. For the Wachowskis, perhaps, worse was still to come.

Initial response to the concluding film of the *Matrix* trilogy was also negative. Fans who spent those years wrestling with the big questions from *The Matrix* only to find that *Reloaded* raised even more, were sometimes disappointed that few answers were apparently forthcoming in *The Matrix Revolutions*. This comment is typical of many posted on one of the thousands of web pages devoted to these films:[168]

> *Matrix Revolutions* makes no sense whatsoever ... it doesn't have any good action, it's too emotional and explains absolutely nothing. It is a very disappointing ending to the trilogy.

The critics weren't impressed either. Glenn Whipp of the *Los Angeles Daily News* accused them of being 'largely devoid of the kind of wonder and storytelling that hooked us the first time.'[169] 'The razor-sharp logic and exhilarating imagination of the first film has been replaced, in the two sequels, by a pile of quasi-religious symbolism and mythological claptrap that adds up to a whole lot of nothing.'[170] Peter Travers agreed in *Rolling Stone*: 'At the risk of understatement, *The Matrix Revolutions* sucks. It's not that the final chapter in the trilogy doesn't have stunts and visual wizardry to drop your jaw. It's just that it all adds up to a supersize nothing: "the big bubkis", to lift a bit of Yiddish from the script.'[171]

Cosmo Landesman in *The Sunday Times* (9 November 2003) accused *Reloaded* of being 'just another undistinguished blockbuster, built on special effects, all bang-bang brawn and no brains,' before going on to write that '*Revolutions* is worse ... [it] never addresses or resolves the philosophical questions posed at the beginning of the trilogy.'

---

[168] fantasticadaily.com/movie_review.php?aID=867

[169] u.dailynews.com/Stories/0,1413,211~24684~1743733,00.html

[170] www.miami.com/mld/miamiherald/entertainment/movies/7180237.htm

[171] www.rollingstone.com/reviews/movie/review.asp?mid=2047748

Like most reviews of each part of the *Matrix* trilogy, these critics have, to my mind, failed to understand what's really going on. It's not that *The Matrix Revolutions* isn't without problems, but that the key questions that *The Matrix* raised are *still* central to the Wachowskis' vision. Back in 1999, it was relatively easy to pick up on at least some questions that the brothers were addressing: What is real? What does it mean to be human? Are we free? But many questions only surfaced after watching the film three or four times – when you finally begin to understand what's going on.

After four years it seems that the critics (and some fans) have got bored of the questions. Apparently all they want is some nice, neat – but extremely cool and action-packed – answers to the riddles. They've forgotten that if part one of this story needed serious thought, perhaps part three does too. Those critics who say that *The Matrix* could be watched simply as an action movie fell at the first hurdle of the real course that the brothers had set. The Wachowskis conceived of this story as a trilogy from the outset – not an 'original' with two sequels as afterthoughts. They should be considered together.

Some critics seem to have forgotten this. Rene Rodriguez again: '*Revolutions* conclusively proves that the Wachowskis had little substantial to add to the premise of the 1999 original – our reality is an artificial construct designed by the machines that have enslaved us – when they decided to spin out *The Matrix* into a trilogy.'[172]

A trilogy can be examined in terms of its parts (as we've done in Part One) but can only really be

[172] www.miami.com/mld/miamiherald/entertainment/movies/7180237.htm

understood as a whole (as we've attempted to do in Part Two). 'The brothers' are still telling the same story and tackling the same questions – some of the most important we can consider. The Wachowskis' angle on them from beginning to end deserves to be thought through very carefully.

Unity in diversity

As we've already seen, there are many different answers out there to *The Matrix*'s big questions, and the brothers have cleverly woven many of them into their entire story. Andy and Larry Wachowski wanted to tell a big, powerful story. Far from giving us a mishmash of unconnected philosophical and religious morsels, they have deliberately integrated elements of the most potent stories from human culture into the story that they wanted to tell. Steve Couch referred in chapter 2 to Joseph Campbell's idea of the monomyth – the idea that all hero myths follow the same basic pattern.[173] This may well have shaped the Wachowskis' story telling[174] and given them the freedom to incorporate elements from elsewhere.

Campbell later claimed that all myths basically communicate the ideas of a strand of Hinduism – a worldview which seems to have no problem absorbing just about every other religious perspective. Campbell expressed it as, 'All religions are true, but none are literal.' The films can therefore include elements from many different religions without worrying about being particularly consistent with any one of them. There's no

[173] Joseph Campbell, *The Hero with a Thousand Faces*, (Pantheon Books, 1949).

[174] See www.jitterbug.com/origins/myth.html

real surprise in the fact that, although the Christian elements remain to the fore (the Wachowski brothers know their North American culture after all), at the end of the saga it is the Hindu perspective which comes to dominate. The combination of monomyth and Hinduism, together with postmodern philosophy, incorporates everything else. Rather like Agent Smith, then!

Everything becomes integrated into one main story – the story of Neo and his quest to find out the truth about the Matrix, to find genuine freedom, and to find peace by finding out who he really is.

Searching for reality, truth and meaning
The nature of the Matrix world

One of the most discussed questions has been, 'What is real? How do you define "real"?' In answering his own question, Morpheus limited his (and our) focus to what we perceive to be physical reality: 'If you're talking about what you can feel, what you can smell, taste and see, then "real" is simply electrical signals interpreted by your brain.' While some of the deeper questions may have eluded us on our first viewing, not many people will have left the cinema without asking themselves, 'Could we be in the Matrix? How do we know that the world is real?'

At one level we don't know. If all our information comes from within the system of our physical world, we can't tell if it's genuine or not. But a little thought about the physics of a 'neural-interactive simulation' like the Matrix shows that it's not possible.

Suppose you are in a pod being fed data through the plug in your head. Simulating what you can 'see' in one direction isn't hard – given reasonable processing power the machines can make it look perfect. Compression techniques mean they don't need to fill in every last detail. Not at first, anyway. The problem comes when you move your head. First, the machines must create the physical sensation of moving your head. Then they have to rapidly generate the changing field of view. They don't know in advance which way you'll move your head, so the data for all fields of view has to be stored somewhere, ready for use.

What if you focus on something – some skin on your hand perhaps. You look closely at it; and all kinds of extra detail need filling in. You move closer – more detail. You get a magnifying glass – more fields of view, more objects, more physical sensation, more detail. Then out with the microscope – and a scalpel to remove a slither of skin – and down to the lab to put it into an electron microscope. Every last detail right down to the smallest scale we can view needs to be there just in case. And we've barely allowed for the physiological and tactile sensations in all of this. We've not mentioned sound or smell or taste. We've not included all the other thoughts that rush through your brain.

Now repeat that for every other person. The amount of information escalates at a phenomenal rate because the system has to allow for all the possibilities. Compression techniques don't work when you can zoom in more and more – the data has to be there ready. It's a problem called *combinatorial explosion*. The only solution to the problem is to use a 'real' world – you need exactly as much data as what we believe to be the real world already contains. If you believe in reality at all, you can be confident that we're in it – it's not a computer simulation.

What reality?

The catch is, 'if you believe in reality at all.' As we've already seen in chapter 7, some postmodern thinkers like Baudrillard deny that it exists – or at least, that we have access to it. Within the context of the films (where we excuse the machines from having to cope with combinatorial explosion!) we can be no more certain that the world of Zion, underground tunnels and machine cities is real than we could be about the Matrix world. How is it that Neo can stop the Sentinels as he could in *The Matrix*? How can he see the code in this other world (a different type of code in a different colour, but code nonetheless, I suspect)?

As we saw in chapter 7, without reality, without truth, there is no possibility of meaning or purpose or value. Yet we crave these things; we long for reality. Could it be that the 'splinter in our minds' points to a greater reality? Freud claimed that belief in God was merely a longing for a father figure projected onto a cosmic plane – there is no God because human beings are really only wanting a father when they talk about God. But isn't it at least plausible that we long for 'Ultimate Reality' because he is there and we really were created to be in a relationship with him? Does thirst imply that 'water' is only expressing our longing for refreshment? Or are we thirsty because we need something that really does exist? Maybe it's the same with God.

Searching for freedom

As Tom Price pointed out in chapter 11, the search for redemption in one form or another is central to all powerful films. This overlaps in various ways with each of the searches on which I am focusing in this chapter. But there is a particularly strong connection with the search for freedom. Redemption means 'to buy back' – originally it referred to buying a slave's freedom.

Everyone wants freedom. Thomas Anderson wanted to be free of the splinter in his mind, but Cypher wanted to return to the Matrix so he could be free to indulge himself. Morpheus instructs Neo to 'free [his] mind'. The ethos of the rebels is to free people from the Matrix. The inhabitants of Zion want to be free from the threat of attack.

Choice, the issue is choice

However, as Peter Williams explores in chapter 9, much of the trilogy, particularly *Reloaded*, explores the question of whether people can ever be free, regardless of whether they're in or out of the Matrix. The Merovingian is fixated with the idea of causality; for him it is the only constant, the only universal. In his mind, there is nothing more than deterministic processes: 'Where some see coincidence, I see consequence; where some see chance, I see cause.'

Agent Smith evidently finds the concept of freedom somewhat alien. When he meets Neo again in *Reloaded*, he tells him, 'We're not here because we're free. We're here because we're *not* free. There is no escaping reason; no denying purpose.' The Architect strongly implies that Neo has no real choice but has been entirely driven by circumstances. Rama-Kandra is simply working through his karma: 'It is a way of saying "What I am here to do." '

It's no surprise that computer programs think in this way. But the humans generally don't see it that way. Neo, in particular, comes to recognise that the issue of choice is central. In *The Matrix*, he faces a fork in his path again and again – one option opens up new possibilities and takes him towards freedom, the other maintains the control of the Matrix. Follow the white rabbit or sleep. Be a good employee of Meta Cortechs or find a new job. Climb to the gantry or face the Agents. Live the life of Thomas Anderson or of Neo the hacker ('One of these lives has a future, and one of them does not,' says Agent Smith). Trust Trinity or go down a familiar road. Red pill or blue pill. Stark choices face Neo throughout his journey.

The Oracle turns out to be the one of the few AIs to recognise that choice is real, and offers Neo the choice of trusting her or not. She would appear to be the intuitive program mentioned by the Architect, who realised that humans needed a measure of choice. At the very end of the trilogy, having played her 'dangerous game', she has evidently secured a genuine freedom for all humans – they can leave the Matrix if they wish.

Because I choose to

The Wachowskis are arguing passionately for freedom. Apparently, the really important thing about human beings (and, perhaps, any genuinely intelligent AI) is that we can choose. In their final showdown, Agent Smith wrestles with Neo's determination to keep on fighting: 'You must be able to see it, Mr Anderson. You must know it by now. You can't win. It's pointless to keep fighting. Why, Mr Anderson? Why? Why do you persist?' Neo's reply is simple and to the point: 'Because I choose to.'

It's the choosing itself that seems to be all-important. It's a very existential approach: authenticate yourself as a person by choosing – *what* you choose is immaterial. This fits with the way Andy and Larry Wachowski have incorporated the ideas of so many worldviews within the films. It doesn't matter which perspective you have on the trilogy – Christian or Gnostic, Hindu or Buddhist – you choose. This is entirely consistent with the post-modern insistence that every view has equal value.

Freedom and pseudo-freedom

People long to be free – to be physically free (no con-straints on what we do), intellectually free (making up our own minds) and morally free (making our own deci-sions about right and wrong). We want to choose.

Humans first embraced this kind of freedom in Genesis 3. It's the account of the first rebellion against God in which humans fell for the line that God doesn't have our best interests at heart, and is denying us free-dom. Eve and Adam chose to ignore the one constraint from God on what they could do.[175] They wanted to choose what to think. They wanted to decide what was good for them. The tragic irony is that they had extraor-dinary freedom – to eat from any tree except one. They knew all they needed to know and more – they even had easy access to God who could enlighten them further. They didn't need to know about good and evil because they lived in the blissful state of only knowing good. And when they exercised their freedom in the one for-bidden way, they ended up losing it. Nothing would ever be the same – they threw away their home and their easy existence because they had cut themselves off

---

[175] 'You are free to eat from any tree in the garden; but you must not eat from the tree of the knowledge of good and evil, for when you eat of it you will surely die.' Genesis 2:16-17 (*NIV*).

from the source. By choosing to make up their own minds, they lost their relationship with the source of all truth. By choosing to define their own morality they discovered that they had come to know good and evil – from the inside. They were no longer simply good, but had to contend with the reality of evil within them. They became slaves, locked into their pattern of rebellion against God. They wrecked their relationships with God, with their environment and with each other. Bad choice.

We are free to choose knowing God or rejecting him – but it's not an arbitrary choice. Choosing a relationship with God opens up a new life to us. Real freedom can only come though a relationship with our creator because that's what he created us for. Choosing to keep on rebelling against him keeps us locked within the system of life (or rather, death) as we know it. One of these lives has a future; one of them does not.

Searching for peace

Intimately connected with the search for freedom is the search for peace. Peace is the goal of all the rebels, and of the One in particular whose 'coming would hail the destruction of the Matrix, end the war, bring freedom to [the] people.' Although we discover in *The Matrix Reloaded* that the Oracle is a program and possibly part of the system of control, in *Revolutions* she tells Neo, 'I want the same thing you do ... and I'm willing to go as far as you are to get it.'

Peace is so great a prize that most of the rebels would willingly give their lives for it. It's more important than freeing people from the Matrix since, as Morpheus tells us in *The Matrix*, many of those whose bodies are in the pods are too established within their virtual world to be freed. The lives of Matrix denizens are expendable for the sake of defeating the machines. Peace, the rebels believe, cannot be achieved without the Matrix being destroyed.

Synergy

After heading in that direction for the first two films and most of the third, the final dénouement comes as something of a surprise at first viewing. The Matrix apparently continues. But it's not the same Matrix – it's the seventh, a new Matrix after the previous version *had* been destroyed.[176] It looks the same but it's a new world order. The end of the war has come about, not through the defeat of the machines, but through an agreement between them and Neo to abandon hostilities. This has struck some people as a rather lame ending. Hadn't we expected Neo to singlehandedly destroy the machines somehow? It was a naïve expectation, if so. What could he do – pull the plug out? And what would have happened to everyone in the Matrix if he had destroyed the machines? The importance of the conversation between Neo and Councillor Hamann in *The Matrix Reloaded* takes on fresh significance when you think about what Neo does achieve:

> Hamann: Down here, sometimes I think about all those people still plugged into the Matrix, and when I look at these machines I ... I can't help but think that in some way, we are plugged into them.

[176] In Christianity and Judaism, seven is representative of completeness. According to Hinduism, we are in the seventh cycle of the world's destruction and recreation.

Neo: But we control these machines; they don't control us.

Hamann: Of course not. How could they? The idea is pure nonsense. But it does make one wonder just what is control?

Neo: If we wanted, we could shut these machines down.

Hamann: [Of] course! That's it! You hit it! That's control, isn't it? If we wanted, we could smash them to bits! Although, if we did, we'd have to consider what would happen to our lights, our heat, our air –

Neo: So we need machines and they need us. Is that your point, Councillor?

Hamann: No, no point. Old men like me don't bother making points. There's no point.

Neo's interaction with programs perhaps also influenced his approach. He realises that he can still trust the Oracle even though she's not human. Perhaps he even trusts her more, since she must understand far more of what's going on behind the scenes than he ever could. His encounter with Sati and her parents on Mobil Ave station is important too. Neo is completely thrown by Rama-Kandra's expression of his love for his daughter. Neo protests that love is a human emotion. 'No, it is a word,' Rama-Kandra replies. 'What matters is the connection it implies. I see you are in love. Can you tell me what you would give to hang on to that connection?' Neo would, of course, give anything. But if these programs are so fully sentient that connections between individuals matter in this way, they cannot be all bad. How *could* he destroy these relationships?

So the end of the war comes through achieving some

balance or harmony. It suits the machines because they don't have to expend energy dealing with terrorists. The humans can go along with it because in the seventh Matrix they can choose whether to stay in it or leave. An age of synergy and mutual co-operation could be ahead. It is perhaps the most positive ending there could be.

Harmony

However, it is interesting that this final harmony is set in the context of Hinduism. The final fight between Neo and Agent Smith takes place while a piece of music, *Neodammerung*[177] (Neo's twighlight), is playing. The Sanskrit words are taken from the Upanishads. The same words are used in *Navras*, the music for the closing credits of *Matrix Revolutions*:

> From delusion lead me to Truth.
> From darkness lead me to Light.
> From death lead me to immortality.[178]
> He who knows both knowledge and action,
> with action overcomes death
> and with knowledge reaches immortality.[179]
> In him are woven the sky and the earth
> and all the regions of the air, and in him
> rest the mind and all the powers of life.
> Know him as the ONE and leave aside all
> other words. He is the bridge of immortality.[180]
> Beyond the senses is the mind, and beyond
> the mind is reason, its essence. Beyond

---

[177] Written by Ben Watkins and Don Davis. There is a nod to Wagner's *Götterdammerung* here.

[178] Brhadaranyaka Upanishad 1.3.28 – all translations from *The Upanishads* translated by Juan Mascaro (Penguin Books, 1965).

[179] Isa Upanishad 11.

[180] Mundaka Upanishad 2.2.5.

reason is the Spirit in man, and beyond this is
the Spirit of the Universe, the evolver of all.[181]
When the five senses and the mind are still,
and reason itself rests in silence, then
begins the Path supreme.[182]
And when he is seen in his immanence and
transcendence, then the ties that have
bound the heart are unloosened, the doubts
of the mind vanish, and the law of Karma
works no more.[183]

Navras also includes the Hindu mantra, *aum shanti shanti shanti*. *Aum* is an ancient Sanskrit word which is supposed to be the sound of the universe. The universe in Hinduism is, of course, basically an illusion – the web of Maya. The Upanishads explain that *aum* represents the world and its parts – including past, present and future. *Shanti* means peace, and the mantra is an invocation of peace. These would seem to be providing some interpretive grid for understanding what's happening in these final scenes.

The resolution to the plot is achieving balance. There are two pairs of great, intractable opposing forces in the *Matrix* trilogy: humans *versus* machines, and Neo *versus* Agent Smith. The latter pair, the Oracle informs Neo, are inextricably linked: 'He is you, your opposite, your negative – the result of the equations trying to balance themselves out.' Not for nothing is she wearing yin yang earrings as she announces this – it is the eastern symbol for balance and harmony. Humans and machines achieve balance through harmony; Neo and

---

[181] Katha Upanishad 6.7.
[182] Katha Upanishad 6.10.
[183] Mundaka Upanishad 2.2.8.

Agent Smith achieve balance through effectively can-
celling each other out. When Neo allows Agent Smith to
take him over, he opens the door to Agent Smith
destroying himself by absorbing his opposite.

Shalom

Attractive though this balance is, I wonder if this is
enough of a solution to the yearning for peace that
characterises human beings. It's clearly a good thing to
try to live in some kind of harmony with others but the
mutual destruction of yourself and your negative (if you
could ever find it) is not a very practical idea. It's worth
noting again at this point that the *Matrix* trilogy is
attempting to synthesise both eastern and western spirituality and philosophy (again, something Joseph
Campbell was keen on). As we have seen already,
Hinduism easily accommodates almost any other worldview: 'Hindus believe that no particular religion teaches
the only way to salvation above all others, but that all
genuine religious paths are facets of God's Pure Love
and Light, deserving tolerance and understanding.'[184]
The Hindu approach to harmony, therefore, is, at least
partly, to set aside or downplay the differences and tension. It meshes very easily with postmodernism.

But Christians believe that Jesus – uniquely – is God
incarnate and is the ultimate revelation of God. When
Jesus claimed that he is 'the way, the truth and the life,'
it was an absolute, exclusive claim. 'No one,' he contin-
ued, 'comes to the Father except through me.'[185] Either
that claim is true or it isn't. It can't just be absorbed into
a worldview that claims 'no particular religion teaches

---

[184] From the Hindu website www.himalayanacademy.com/basics/point/index. html
[185] John 14:6 (*NIV*).

the only way to salvation above all others.' If Jesus' claim *is* true, it cuts through that particular Hindu claim – they can't both be true. If Jesus' claim *is not* true, then Christianity cannot even be considered a 'genuine religious path'. If Jesus is telling the truth, there is no alternative way to knowing peace with God. If Jesus *is not* telling the truth, he is no way to knowing peace with God. That's not to say that other religious views, including Hinduism, don't offer any moral guidance or spiritual insight, but that they cannot be finally true if Christianity is, and *vice versa*.

Jesus Christ, through his sacrificial death on the cross – dying the death we deserve for our rebellion against God – offers us peace with God. Ultimate peace. The biblical concept is the Hebrew word, *shalom* – it's a much bigger concept than we normally think of when we talk about peace. It's not a balance of opposites or a cessation of hostilities, but a state of all-encompassing well-being because we are in a right relationship with the creator.

Searching for self-understanding

Peace with God – *shalom* – results, ultimately, in the possibility of peace with others, and with yourself. This is one of the deepest longings of the human heart. It's the answer to our inward turmoil, the tensions we struggle with, the guilt and shame we privately feel, and the lack of certainty about who we are and what life is all about.

Agent Smith's characterisations of humans are always graphic and never positive. Having called humanity a virus in *The Matrix*, in *Revolutions* he perceives in the blinded Neo something representative of all of us. As he watches him stagger with pain, crashing into the walls, he calls him a 'blind messiah ... You're a symbol for all of your kind, Mr Anderson – helpless, pathetic, just waiting to be put out of your misery.' Well, there's some truth there. But Neo, while he may be physically in a mess, is beginning to see things ever clearer. It's not just that he can see the code of the real world, but that he has been discovering who he really is.

Throughout the *Matrix* trilogy, Neo has been on a journey to self-knowledge. When he first meets the Oracle, she points to a plaque on her kitchen wall and explains to Neo that, 'It's Latin. Means, "Know thyself." ' She reminds him of it in *Matrix Revolutions* when Neo quizzes her about why she hadn't told him all she knew. From his uncertain beginnings as troubled computer hacker Thomas Anderson, through to his complete self-confidence at the end, Neo has been working towards peace with himself.

He's made progress through some crisis moments and some dawning realisations, but I believe that it is this quest more than any other which is at the heart of the *Matrix* trilogy. His search for reality and truth, his quest for freedom and peace for Zion, are part of his journey towards discovering who he really is. The search for meaning or purpose is part of this. And it's a journey that we are on too. Like Neo, we want to feel at peace with ourselves, regardless of circumstances, by knowing who we really are.

All of our attempts at self-discovery, at achieving something, at becoming happy, are all expressions of our inbuilt drive to know *shalom*. With their inclusion of diverse religious and philosophical ideas, the Wachowskis could be saying that everything is open to us, there's something for everyone. The important thing is to *choose*. The trouble is, in a postmodern world where no ground is firm enough to stand on, a random choice just for the sake of choosing, or an attempt to harmonise competing views, will leave you in a world of illusion. Just like the *Matrix* trilogy, which never finally answers the question of what is real. But real *shalom* is on offer. Real peace with ourselves comes, ultimately, only in the context of peace with our creator through the real historical death and resurrection of Jesus, his Son.

Back in the first film, Cypher wanted to return to live inside the Matrix. He couldn't cope with the challenges of life in the 'real' world. He wanted nothing more than to live an easy life with nothing troubling him – a life of pleasure and entertainment, of status and wealth. But a life not based on truth. For Trinity and the others, though, 'It's the question which drives us.' The question which Cypher's choice raised confronts each of us: which is better – to live a comfortable life that is based on a lie, or do whatever it takes to find the truth? We're back to red pill or blue pill. Where we go from here is a choice I leave to you.

Bibliography

Visit the *Damaris* Culture Watch website at www.damaris.org/ cw/ for a wealth of up-to-the-minute material examining the ideas behind popular culture.

General background reading

Wachowski, Andy and Larry, *The Matrix: The Shooting Script* (Newmarket Press, 2001)

The Official Matrix Web Site at http://whatisthematrix.warner bros.com/

Godawa, Brian, *Hollywood Worldviews* (InterVarsity Press, 2002)

Thacker, Anthony, *A Closer Look at Science Fiction* (Kingsway, 2001)

Irwin, William (ed.), *The Matrix and Philosophy* (Open Court, 2002)

Lamm, Spencer *et al*, *The Art of "the Matrix"* (Titan Books, 2000)

Yeffeth, Glenn (ed.), *Taking the Red Pill* (Summersdale, 2003)

Recommended background viewing

The Animatrix (Warner Bros., 2003) (15)

Ghost in the Shell (Manga Video, 2000) (15)

Akira (Manga Entertainment, 2003) (15)

Ninja Scroll (Manga Video, 2000) (18)

Here is a range of recommended resources listed by subject:

Truth, knowledge, value and postmodernism

Beilby, James and David K. Clark, 'A Brief Introduction to the Theory of Knowledge' at www.gospelcom.net/rzim/publications/ essay_arttext.php?id=12

Clark, James Kelly, 'How Real People Believe – a Defence of Reformed Epistemology' at www.modernreformation.org/mr98/ janfeb/mr9801defense.html

Descartes, René, *Meditations on First Philosophy* at www.cola. wright.edu/DesCartes/Meditations.html

Koons, Robert C., 'The Relativistic Bog: Two Sources of Knowledge about God' at www.gradresources.org/worldview_ articles/bog. shtml

Kreeft, Peter, 'A Refutation of Moral Relativism' (mp3 audio file) at www.peterkreeft.com/audio/05_relativism/refutation-of-relativism.mp3

Plantinga, Alvin, 'Theism, Atheism and Rationality' at www.leaderu. com/truth/3truth02.html

Beckwith, Francis J. and Gregory Koukl, *Relativism: Feet Firmly Planted in Mid-Air* (Baker, 2001)

Chamberlain, Paul, *Can We Be Good Without God?* (InterVarsity Press, 1996)

Copan, Paul, *'True for You, But not for Me': Defeating the Slogans that leave Christians Speechless* (Bethany House, 1998)

Groothuis, Douglas, *Truth Decay* (InterVarsity Press, 2000)

Honeysett, Marcus, *Meltdown* (InterVarsity Press, 2002)

Plantinga, Alvin, *Warranted Christian Belief* (Oxford, 2000)

Jean Baudrillard

Feluga, Dino, 'Modules on Baudrillard: On Postmodernity' from *Introductory Guide to Critical Theory*, updated 25 June 2003, Purdue University –www.sla.purdue.edu/academic/engl/theory/postmodernism/modules/baudrillardpostmodernity.html

A Rough Chronology Of Jean Baudrillard's Thoughts On The World at www.geneseo.edu/~bicket/panop/baudrillard.htm

Baudrillard, Jean, translated by Sheila Glaser, *Simulacra and Simulation* (University of Michigan Press, 1994)

Worldviews

Bryan College, *Worldview Studies* at www.bryan.edu/worldview/

Netland, Harold A., 'Worldview Criteria' at www.gradresources.org/worldview_articles/worldview_criteria.shtml

Solomon, Jerry, 'Worldviews' at www.probe.org/docs/w-views.html

World View Test Site at www.geocities.com/worldview_3/

Geisler, Norman L. and William D. Watkins, *Worlds Apart: A Handbook On World Views* (Baker, 1989)

Sire, James W., *The Universe Next Door* (InterVarsity Press, 1997)

Artificial intelligence and the mind-body problem

Damaris Center for Soul and Consciousness Studies at www.damaris.org/dcscs/index2.htm

Dembski, William A., 'Are We Spiritual Machines?' at www.designinference.com/documents/1999.10.spiritual_machines.htm

Dembski, William A., 'The Primacy of the First Person: Reply to Ray Kurzweil' at www.designinference.com/documents/2002.07.kurzweil_reply.htm

Dembski, William A., 'The Act of Creation: Bridging Transcendence and Immanence' at www.designinference.com/documents/1998.08.act_of_creation.htm

Dembski, William A., 'Challenging Materialism's "Chokehold" on Neuroscience' at www.designinference.com/documents/2003.02.Schwartz_Review.htm

Descartes, René, *Meditations on First Philosophy* at www.cola.wright.edu/DesCartes/Meditations.html

Hasker, William, 'How Not to be a Reductivist' at www.iscid.org/papers/Hasker_NonReductivism_103103.pdf

Willard, Dallas, 'Knowledge and Naturalism' at www.dwillard.org/articles/artview.asp?artID=64

Williams, Peter S., 'Why Naturalists Should Mind About Physicalism, and Vice Versa' at www.damaris.org/dcscs/readingroom/2000/williams1.htm

Gilder, George and Jay Richards, *Are We Spiritual Machines? Ray Kurzweil vs. the Critics of Strong A.I.* (Discovery Institute, 2002)

Kelly, Kevin, *Out of Control: The New Biology of Machines* (Fourth Estate, 1995)

Assessing naturalism (cf. the anti-naturalism argument from reason)
ARN at www.arn.org/

The Anti-Naturalism Page at http://startthinking.homestead.com/naturalism1.html

Hasker, William, 'How Not to be a Reductivist' at www.iscid.org/papers/Hasker_NonReductivism_103103.pdf

Koons, Robert C., 'The Incompatibility of Naturalism and Scientific Realism' at www.leaderu.com/offices/koons/docs/natreal.html

Plantinga, Alvin, 'An Evolutionary Argument Against Naturalism' at http://hisdefense.org/articles/ap001.html

Listen to Plantinga lecturing on his anti-naturalism argument at www.hisdefense.org/audio/ap_001.ram

Willard, Dallas, 'Knowledge and Naturalism' at www.dwillard.org/articles/artview.asp?artID=64

Behe, Michael J., William A. Dembski and Stephen C. Meyer, *Science and Evidence for Design in the Universe* (Ignatius, 2000)

Craig, William Lane and J. P. Moreland (eds), *Naturalism: A Critical Analysis* (Routledge, 2001)

Dembski, William A., *No Free Lunch: Why Specified Complexity Cannot be Purchased without Intelligence* (Rowman & Littlefield, 2001)

Hasker, William, *The Emergent Self* (Cornell University Press, 1999)

Lewis, C. S., *Miracles* (Fount, 1998)

McGrath, Alister, *The Re-Enchantment of Nature: Science, Religion and the Human Sense of Wonder* (Hodder & Stoughton, 2002)

Moreland, J. P., *Scaling the Secular City* (Baker, 1987)

Moreland, J. P. and Rae, Scott B., *Body & Soul: Human Nature & the Crisis in Ethics* (InterVarsity Press, 2000)

Ratzsch, Del, *Science & Its Limits: The Natural Sciences in Christian Perspective* (Apollos, 2000)

Ward, Keith, *God, Chance & Necessity* (OneWorld, 1996)

The anti-naturalism argument from reason
Hasker, William, 'How Not to be a Reductivist' at www.iscid.org/papers/Hasker_NonReductivism_103103.pdf

Koons, Robert C., 'Lewis on Naturalism' at www.leaderu.com/offices/koons/docs/natreal.html

Koons, Robert C., 'The Incompatibility of Naturalism and Scientific Realism' at www.leaderu.com/offices/koons/docs/natreal.html

Koukl, Gregory, 'Dominoes, Determinism, and Naturalism' at www.str.org/free/commentaries/evolution/dominosd.htm

Lovell, Steven, 'C.S. Lewis' Case Against Naturalism' at http://myweb.tiscali.co.uk/cslphilos/CSLnat.htm

Plantinga, Alvin, 'An Evolutionary Argument Against Naturalism' at http://hisdefense.org/articles/ap001.html

Willard, Dallas, 'Knowledge and Naturalism' at www.dwillard.org/articles/artview.asp?artID=64

Williams, Peter S, 'Why Naturalists Should Mind About Physicalism, and Vice Versa' at www.damaris.org/dcscs/readingroom/2000/williams1.htm

Interview with Dr. Victor Reppert at http://go.qci.tripod.com/Reppert-interview.htm

Hasker, William, *The Emergent Self* (Cornell University Press, 1999)

Lewis, C. S, *Miracles* (Fount, 1998)

Moreland, J. P., *Scaling the Secular City* (Baker, 1987)

Plantinga, Alvin, *Warrant and Proper Function* (Oxford, 2003)

Reppert, Victor, *C. S. Lewis' Dangerous Idea* (InterVarsity Press, 2003)

Prophecy

Bloom, John A., 'Is Fulfilled Prophecy of Value for Scholarly Apologetics?' at www.apologetics.com/default.jsp?bodycontent=/articles/biblical_apologetics/bloom-prophecy.html

Totton, R., 'Prophecy Proves the Bible' at www.geocities.com/Athens/Aegean/8830/prophecy.html

Geivett, R. Douglas and Gary R. Habermas (eds), *In Defence of Miracles* (Apollos, 1997)

Muncaster, Ralph O., *Does the Bible Predict the Future?* (Harvest House, 2000)

Foreknowledge

Craig, William Lane, 'Tachyons, Time Travel, and Divine Omniscience' at www.leaderu.com/offices/billcraig/docs/tachyons.html

Craig, William Lane, 'Divine Foreknowledge and Newcomb's Paradox' at www.leaderu.com/offices/billcraig/docs/newcomb.html

Holt, Tim, 'The Argument from Future Facts' at www.philosophyofreligion.info/futurefacts.html

Koukl, Gregory, 'What Determines the Future?' at www.str.org/free/commentaries/theology/future.htm

Copan, Paul, *"That's Just Your Interpretation": Responding to Skeptics Who Challenge Your Faith* (Baker Books, 2001)

Beilby, James and Paul R. Eddy, (ed.), *Divine Foreknowledge: 4 Views* (InterVarsity Press, 2001)

The historical reliability of the New Testament

Copan, Paul, 'You Can't Trust the Gospels. They're Unreliable' at www.countercult.com/r14ac.html

France, R. T., 'The Gospels as Historical Sources for Jesus, the Founder of Christianity' at www.leaderu.com/truth/1truth21.html

Habermas, Gary R., 'Why I Believe the New Testament is Historically Reliable' at www.apologetics.com/default.jsp?bodycontent=/articles/historical_apologetics/habermas-nt.html

Barnet, Paul, *Is The New Testament Reliable?* (InterVarsity Press, 1986)

Blomberg, Craig L., *The Historical Reliability of the Gospels* (InterVarsity Press, 1987)

Habermas, Gary R., *The Historical Jesus: Ancient Evidence for the Life of Christ* (College Press, 2001)

The historical evidence for Jesus' resurrection

Craig, William Lane at www.leaderu.com/offices/billcraig/menus/index.html

Craig, William Lane, 'Did the Resurrection Really Happen?' at www.gospelcom.net/rzim/radio/easter.shtml (mp3 File)

Habermas, Gary R., 'The Facts Concerning the Resurrection' at www.ankerberg.com/Articles/_PDFArchives/editors-choice/EC3W0302.pdf

Kreeft, Peter and Ronald Tacelli, 'Evidence for the Resurrection of Christ' at http://hometown.aol.com/philvaz/articles/num9.htm

Copan, Paul (ed.), *Will the Real Jesus Please Stand Up? A Debate between William Lane Craig and John Dominic Crossan* (Baker, 1998)

Craig, William Lane, *The Son Rises* (Moody Press, 1981)

Davis, Stephen T., *Risen Indeed* (SPCK, 1993)

Swinburne, Richard, *The Resurrection of God Incarnate* (Oxford, 2002)

Walker, Peter, *The Weekend that Changed the World* (Marshall Pickering, 1999)

Love

Budziszewski, J. *How to Stay Christian in College* (NavPress, 1999)

Kreeft, Peter, *The Best Things in Life* (InterVarsity Press, 1984)

Lewis, C. S., *The Four Loves* (HarperCollins, 2002)

McDowell, Josh and Norman L. Geisler, *Love is Always Right: A Defence of the One Moral Absolute* (Word Publishing, 1996)

Redemption

McGrath, Alister, *Making Sense of the Cross* (InterVarsity Press, 1992)

The systemic anomaly

by Tony Watkins

Your life is the sum of a remainder of an unbalanced equation inherent to the programming of the Matrix. You are the eventuality of an anomaly, which, despite my sincerest efforts, I have been unable to eliminate from what is otherwise a harmony of mathematical precision.

Andy and Larry Wachowski said they wanted to make a film about 'mythology, theology and higher mathematics.' The rest of this book explores something of the mythology and theology in the films, but where is the higher mathematics? For many people, it's not a question worth asking – basic mathematics can be scary enough without starting on the higher stuff. However, two particular aspects of the mathematical influence on this trilogy are worth thinking about by anyone who is interested in the philosophical side of the films.

Chaos

From before the time of Newton until the early years of the twentieth century, scientists and mathematicians tended to assume that the universe was like a vast machine. Modern science had been remarkably successful at identifying the mathematical basis for the workings of the cosmos – and at predicting its future behaviour. The physics of the large-scale world which we experience each day is simple and straightforward (relatively!). It seems to strongly suggest that events are determined by previous events. The movement of the balls on a snooker table is, in principle, entirely predictable if we know how the cue struck the first ball. If everything we see is so rigidly mathematical, it's likely that the entire universe is – mathematical, predictable, deterministic. It puts a strong emphasis on causality.

Then came quantum physics, which soon showed that at the level of sub-atomic particles, like electrons, it was a different story. We could do the mathematics, but there were limits to what we could calculate. In 1927 Heisenberg developed his Uncertainty Principle, which established a fundamental limit to what we could know about one of these particles. We could know where it was, but have no idea about how fast it was travelling. Or we could know its velocity but not its position. Or a bit of both. The theory was impossible to get around. There was a limit to our knowledge and, therefore, a limit to our ability to predict what would happen. We had to start dealing in probabilities instead of certainties.

There was a random element to it too. Because of this fundamental uncertainty, a particle had to be thought of as in several places or states at any one time *until* someone observed it – measured it – in some way. At that moment, the particle had to be in one place, or in one state. Schröedinger had a famous thought experiment (that is, he imagined the scenario rather than carrying it out) involving a cat sealed in a box with some poison. While the lid is on, we would not know whether the cat was alive or dead. It is not until the lid comes off that we know. As far as we are concerned, the cat could be both alive *and* dead until the moment of observation. The idea of causality was becoming difficult. Einstein reacted strongly against this fundamental indeterminacy by saying, 'God does not play dice!'[186] But the tide was shifting from scientists who held such views. This at least partly lies behind the discussions of causality in *The Matrix Revolutions*.

In the 1960s chaos theory was born. Detailed measurements show that unpredictability was everywhere – even in things as apparently regular as the swing of a pendulum. Science had been dealing with simplified versions of reality in order to fit with their belief in complete determinism and causality. Reality was harder to pin down – it's far more complex than school-level physics suggests. Instead of being a huge clockwork machine, the universe is full of chaotic behaviour. Clouds, leaves on trees and coastlines are classic examples of chaotic systems, not regular ones. Yet there appears to be some order on a large scale. Indeed there is. Out of the chaos of the parts of the system comes another level of order. Again chaos theory showed that there were fundamental limits on our ability to predict what would happen. A tiny variation early on in some system can result in vastly different outcomes. Edward Lorenz discovered this while working on mathematical models for weather systems in 1960. Once chaos was identified as a scientific principle, it cropped up everywhere: heartbeats, ferns, cauliflowers, coral reefs, stock market behaviour ... The list seems to be almost endless. Many of these systems are 'self-organising' – a relatively ordered large-scale view results from chaotic behaviour at smaller scales.

---

[186] Einstein first expressed this in a letter to Max Born (4 December 1926) in which he said 'I am convinced that He [God] does not play dice.'

The surprise was that some of these chaotic systems could be described with very simple mathematics. In process of investigating this, a young mathematician named Benoit Mandelbrot studied the graphs produced by these deceptively simple equations, and was amazed to discover the extraordinary shape now known as the Mandelbrot set. The edge of the Mandelbrot set is like a coastline. The closer you look, the more detail you see. In fact, zoom in as much as you like and you always get new detail. What's so surprising when you first do this, is that the shapes and patterns get repeated as different scales over and over again. At whatever scale you're looking, the coastline looks pretty similar to how it looks at any other scale. This is a property known as self-similarity.

Zooming into the Mandelbrot set forms the first part of the title sequence of *The Matrix Revolutions*, (though there may be a brief hint of it at the start of *The Matrix Reloaded*). We briefly see its self-similarity before we zoom into the code. Self-similarity is a strong visual element in the Architect's 'office' in *The Matrix Reloaded*. As Neo puts the key in the lock, the door appears to dissolve before the intense bright light. The light narrows to a point in a view of space from which we are zooming out. Briefly there is the sense of looking closely at the pixels of a television before we discover that we are now looking at a television screen. The Architect's hand taps his minimalist remote control and we see, on multiple screens, Neo standing in front of the same bank of screens, all showing the same image of Neo. We pan around to face Neo looking around. After some discussion we zoom in on one of the screens and then pass through it to look at exactly the same scene – Neo in front of a bank of screens. The same trick is played a few moments later. Each screen shows the same image so there are screens within screens. It's the same self-similarity as any fractal-generated image like the Mandelbrot set.[187]

Incompleteness

The second key mathematical idea behind the *Matrix* trilogy goes back to 1931. The previous decade had been a time of optimism in the western world. Modernism was the dominant outlook in the West and it seemed to be doing extremely well. The Great War – the war to end all wars – was over, science was making extraordinary progress, and people were beginning to enjoy the fruits of a more prosperous era. They didn't realise that the Great Depression was just around the corner. Rationalism – the belief that human reason is the ultimate judge and can sort out any problem – was almost unchallenged. In that context, mathematicians were busy trying to sort out the foundations of their discipline. They were striving for a completely logical, coherent system, and were confident that they would achieve it very soon, despite the difficulties arising through quantum physics.

But then Kurt Gödel published his Incompleteness Theorem, which blew that confidence away. He proved that any formal system – a rule-based, closed system – like mathematics is always, inevitably incomplete. What this means is that, within mathematics (Gödel's primary

---

[187] Interestingly, the technique of zooming through an image on screen is used twice in *The Matrix* – once in the Construct when Morpheus is showing Neo the 'world as it exists today,' and once when Neo has been arrested by the Agents. We see exactly the same bank of screens as in the Architect scene, and zoom through into the interrogation room.

concern), there are always some things that cannot be proved. It is not possible to prove all mathematical axioms based on other axioms. Some of them will remain unprovable truths. These are known as Gödel sentences, and are usually represented as 'G'. It's not just mathematics – this anomaly is inherent to any formal system. That includes the Matrix.[188]

As Morpheus told Neo in *The Matrix*, the Matrix is based on rules – it's a formal system. As such, there must be a Gödel sentence, an anomaly within it. The Architect explained to Neo – in arguably the most mathematical scene of the trilogy – that the One is the result of this anomaly:

Neo: Why am I here?

Architect: Your life is the sum of a remainder of an unbalanced equation inherent to the programming of the Matrix. You are the eventuality of an anomaly, which, despite my sincerest efforts, I have been unable to eliminate from what is otherwise a harmony of mathematical precision. While it remains a burden assiduously avoided, it is not unexpected, and thus not beyond a measure of control. Which has led you, inexorably ... here.

The system of the Matrix must be incomplete, it must have an anomaly. There is no way round it. The anomaly in the programmed world of the Matrix is choice. But this is personified as 'the One' who is not based on or bound by the rules of the system – he has absolute

---

[188] It also includes the physical universe and can be seen as a pointer to the necessary existence of God.

choice within the system, not the limited appearance of choice, which ordinary Matrix denizens have to contend with. This fundamental, unavoidable problem leads, in this case to problems in the entire system:

> Architect: As you are undoubtedly gathering, the anomaly is systemic – creating fluctuations in even the most simplistic equations.

In other words, small changes in some very simple equations within the system get amplified into a chaotic system – it's fractal behaviour: 'the otherwise contradictory systemic anomaly ... if left unchecked might threaten the system itself. Ergo those that refused the program, while a minority, if unchecked, would constitute an escalating probability of disaster.'

The previous Matrices have each been incomplete, and each had the same anomaly, expressed in the form of a person with extraordinary powers. The only way the machines have had of dealing with this inherent flaw has been to remake the Matrix:

> Architect: The function of the One is now to return to the Source, allowing a temporary dissemination of the code you carry, reinserting the prime program ... Failure to comply with this process will result in a cataclysmic system crash, killing everyone connected to the Matrix, which, coupled with the extermination of Zion, will ultimately result in the extinction of the entire human race.

At every reloading of the Matrix, choice is put back to its minimal level, but like a fractal-generated image, it grows and grows, becoming a self-organising system within the system: Zion.[189] But that's not really dealing with the anomaly. The way of dealing with G in a mathematical system is to make it part of the structure of the system – make it one of the unprovable truths on which other things are built. This is what happens at the end of the story. Rather than just starting everything over again as it was before, the peace that Neo achieves means that the anomaly of choice is built into the system as one of its ground rules. This is clear from the conversation between the Oracle and the Architect at the end of *Revolutions*. She wants to be sure that the Architect is going to allow anyone to leave the Matrix if they want to. He confirms that this is the case. Now everyone has the ultimate choice – stay in the system or leave. The One would appear to be now unnecessary in the new Matrix, and the thing shouldn't spiral out of control.

Except, every time you incorporate a Gödel sentence into the system as part of its structure, you create a new system – which has its own anomaly ...

---

[189] I think there are many clues that the 'real' world is really an extended part of the Matrix itself.